Law, Society, Policy

Series Editor: **Rosie Harding**,
University of Birmingham

Law, Society, Policy offers an outlet for high quality, socio-legal research monographs and edited collections with the potential for policy impact.

Also available in the series

Egalitarian Digital Privacy
Image Based Abuse and Beyond
By **Tsachi Keren-Paz**

Fragile Rights
Disability, Public Policy and Social Change
By **Anne Revillard**

Intersex Embodiment
Legal Frameworks Beyond Identity and Disorder
By **Fae Garland** and **Mitchell Travis**

Unsettling Apologies
Critical Writings on Apology from South Africa
Edited by **Melanie Judge** and **Dee Smythe**

Death, Family and the Law
The Contemporary Inquest in Context
By **Edward Kirton-Darling**

Deprivation of Liberty in the Shadows of the Institution
By **Lucy Series**

Women, Precarious Work and Care
The Failure of Family-friendly Rights
By **Emily Grabham**

Pandemic Legalities
Legal Responses to COVID-19 – Justice and Social Responsibility
Edited by **Dave Cowan** and **Ann Mumford**

Find out more at

bristoluniversitypress.co.uk/law-society-policy

Forthcoming

Children's Voices, Family Disputes and Child-Inclusive Mediation
The Right to Be Heard
By **Anne Barlow** and **Jan Ewing**

Adult Social Care Law and Policy
Lessons from the Pandemic
By **Jean McHale** and **Laura Noszlopy**

Sex Worker Rights Activism and the Politics of Rights:
Within and against the Law
By **Katie Cruz**

Find out more at

bristoluniversitypress.co.uk/law-society-policy

JUDITH TOWNEND
LUCY WELSH

OBSERVING JUSTICE

Digital Transparency, Openness and Accountability in Criminal Courts

BRISTOL
UNIVERSITY
PRESS

First published in Great Britain in 2024 by

Bristol University Press
University of Bristol
1–9 Old Park Hill
Bristol
BS2 8BB
UK
t: +44 (0)117 374 6645
e: bup-info@bristol.ac.uk

Details of international sales and distribution partners are available at bristoluniversitypress.co.uk

British Library Cataloguing in Publication Data
A catalogue record for this book is available from the British Library

ISBN 978-1-5292-2867-0 hardcover
ISBN 978-1-5292-2868-7 ePub
ISBN 978-1-5292-2869-4 ePdf

Cover design: Andrew Corbett
Front cover image: iStock/georgeclerk
Bristol University Press use environmentally responsible print partners.
Printed and bound in Great Britain by CPI Group (UK) Ltd, Croydon, CR0 4YY

FSC
www.fsc.org
MIX
Paper | Supporting responsible forestry
FSC® C013604

Contents

Series Editor's Preface

The Law, Society, Policy series publishes high-quality, socio-legal research monographs and edited collections with the potential for policy impact. Cutting across the traditional divides of legal scholarship, Law, Society, Policy offers an interdisciplinary, policy-engaged approach to socio-legal research which explores law in its social and political contexts with a particular focus on the place of law in everyday life.

The series seeks to take an explicitly society-first view of socio-legal studies, with a focus on the ways that law shapes social life, and the constitutive nature of law and society. International in scope, engaging with domestic, international and global legal and regulatory frameworks, texts in the Law, Society, Policy series engage with the full range of socio-legal topics and themes.

About the Authors

Dr Judith Townend is Reader in Digital Society and Justice at the University of Sussex. Having begun her career in journalism, she has written for a wide range of media and academic publications and is affiliated to organisations including The Transparency Project and Connected by Data. Her research focuses on the protection and regulation of public interest journalism and public access to information.

Dr Lucy Welsh is Reader in Criminal Justice and Director of Clinical Legal Education at the University of Sussex. Lucy was a criminal defence and prison law solicitor for ten years before moving into academia full time in 2016. Her research focuses on issues surrounding access to justice, especially in Magistrates' courts or appellate processes.

Acknowledgements

With thanks to Dr Jon Robins, University of Brighton, and the following University of Sussex students for their role in this research: in 2020, Olivia Kapur, Amanda Coldwell, Jorja Hills, and Chloe Simpson; in 2022, Mariama Cordovil Espada Bah, Hannah Bland, Chloe Machado Da Costa Budd, Spencer McDowell, Mimi Webber and Libby Gissing. We also wish to acknowledge the many court and justice observers who have shared their experiences online and informed the ideas in this book. Finally, thank you to the team at Bristol University Press for commissioning and guiding the project.

Acknowledgements

ONE

Introduction: Why We Need to Rethink Approaches to Open Justice in the Criminal Courts

This book is about the principle and practice of open justice in criminal courts in what is often characterised as the 'digital age'. By this we mean the way in which court hearings and information about cases are made publicly accessible in the context of digital and technological advances in the 21st century.

Publicity of court proceedings is deep-rooted in English and common law tradition, with the earliest articulations of open justice found in 17th century legal history (Robertson 2012). The late 18th and early 19th century philosopher Jeremy Bentham is often quoted to explain the rationale for open courts: 'Publicity is the very soul of justice. It is the keenest spur to exertion and the surest of all guards against improbity. It keeps the judge himself while trying under trial'.[1] From another perspective, however, in the words of a former criminal defendant speaking in the early 21st century: 'publicity is a life sentence and it makes it very difficult for you to put it behind you and move on […] with your life and build a home and get on with everything, when it's a click away from people'.[2]

The second perspective has not been given such credence; and the impact of publicity on individuals and communities (with notable exceptions) is surprisingly under-interrogated in academic and policy literature. This book is motivated by a desire to provoke further discussion about this and other tensions surrounding open justice; and informed by the dilemmas and obstacles we have encountered in our own work when trying to access information about the courts.

These concerns include our inability to obtain basic information about cases (especially in the local Magistrates' court during the first national lockdown of the COVID-19 pandemic); our nagging concerns about the 'human impact' of digitised courts data (such as the impact on private lives and on the relationships between court participants) and inequality of access to the justice system (including practical issues with participation that undermine understanding and engagement); and the confusion and inconsistency characterising justice system data management within and beyond England and Wales.

It is also written to encourage law and policy makers to take a deeper and more pragmatic look at how open justice impacts human lives. As we will show, there has often been a noticeable detachment between lofty statements about open justice and the reality for those observing and experiencing the courts day to day. As well as exposing some of the practical challenges for open justice, we consider some of the ideological tensions at play in the realisation of open justice in society and in criminal proceedings.

Until recently, there had been very limited opportunities for members of the public to engage in the development of open justice policy. We were both co-signatories to an open letter in 2020 that raised this issue (Robins 2020). However, in 2021 the House of Commons Justice Committee undertook a welcome Inquiry on open justice and court reporting.[3] The Committee's report reflects our motivation for this book, noting that there is 'confusion over the precise definition of the principle and how it works in practice' (Justice Committee 2022a, p 4).[4] Not all the Committee's recommendations on implementing and expanding open justice have been received positively by the government (Justice Committee 2023), though a wide-ranging public consultation was launched in 2023. While the consultation paper shies away from making firm commitments, and indicates budgetary constraints, it provides a valuable opportunity to present and develop some of the ideas in this book. Though we cannot fully anticipate specific advances in technology in the next decade, we believe there will be a continued relevance to the tensions and potential responses that we identify here.

In this book, we do not favour overly rigid understandings about the aims of open justice either in criminal proceedings or more broadly. Indeed, as Bandes and Feigenson contend, '[c]ommon-law court systems seek to advance a range of values, including inclusivity, dignity, fairness, accuracy, transparency, and the demonstration of state authority' (2020, p 1281), necessitating some flexibility in approaches. We suggest that open justice has a role to play in each of these values. One of our key concerns is that insufficient regard for them has caused the principle and practice of open justice to be overly focussed on the interests of news media organisations.[5] While journalists play an essential role in delivering open justice, they are not the only conduit for sharing information with the public. The result of this narrow focus is that there are procedural and cultural barriers to observing justice. This undermines both the transparency and, by implication, the potential legitimacy of the criminal process.

We explore the meaning of open justice and illustrate that constricted interpretations and application of the principle have obstructed observation by individuals who are not members of the so-called 'accredited' media. We argue – throughout this book – for an expanded understanding of open justice that responds to the needs and challenges of a digital society. Before we proceed further, it is appropriate to highlight why we have chosen Magistrates' courts as a focal point (particularly in Chapters Two and Three), though we hope that much of what we say could be transferred into other criminal and civil jurisdictions. Indeed, we contend that cross-jurisdictional comparisons are vital to improving open justice practice.[6]

In the first six months of 2022, Magistrates' courts in England and Wales received 603,049 cases and, during the same time frame, Crown Courts received 49,172 cases (Ministry of Justice 2022d). This gulf in case receipts is no anomaly. For many years, Crown Courts have processed far fewer cases each year than Magistrates' courts (Welsh et al 2021), reflecting the fact that Crown Courts deal with only the most serious criminal offences. Consequently, the court that most members of the public are most likely to encounter is the Magistrates' court. Despite this fact, Magistrates' courts are infrequently the subject of extensive academic research (Dadomo and Bell 2006; Welsh 2022), and media outlets tend to focus their resources on reporting the detail of Crown Court cases, sometimes relying only on court listing details in the Magistrates' court for information rather than attending hearings in person (for example, *The Swindon Advertiser* 2019; Chamberlain et al 2021). This reporting behaviour appears to reflect a longstanding (and, we believe, erroneous) belief that Magistrates' courts deal only with trivial matters (McBarnet 1981) of little wider importance. Further, Magistrates' courts are not courts of record, and hearings are not routinely recorded. Therefore, while Magistrates' courts are where most criminal justice is administered, and specific provisions are made about open justice in the Criminal Procedure Rules (Crim PR) and Criminal Practice Directions (Crim PD), much of what happens there is under interrogated as a part of open justice. This, we argue, has implications for transparency and accountability in the criminal process. We, therefore, seek to bring debates about open justice and Magistrates' courts into much sharper focus.

Interrogating 'open justice'

The concept of 'open justice' is highly prominent in popular culture and news media; it is what allows the publication and broadcast of journalists' court reports and the stylised artists' sketches in pastel, and since at least 2010, the live tweeting of trials in England and Wales (Oliver 2010). Case law about open justice has considered issues pertaining to publishing judgments, public accessibility of courts, and on the ability of the news media to attend and report proceedings;[7] the latter for the pragmatic reason that it is usually traditional media organisations which have brought and resourced cases pursuing access to hearings and documents. We take a broad view of open justice that looks beyond the news media as a proxy for transparency and accountability. The Justice Committee (2022a) received several submissions that referred to open justice broadly conceived, in relation to transparency of court administration, data collection issues, accessibility of court hearings and court documents, and the ways that courts communicate with the public. We advocate in favour of open justice as a mechanism of justice system accountability, in that open justice can 'ensure that the public can reach its own judgment on whether the courts are delivering justice' (Justice Committee 2022a, p 7). This check operates at a systemic level, as well as in terms of individual cases. That is, an approach of open justice allows scrutiny of the way in which the system is functioning in general, as well as individual court users to understand their case (and if necessary, access the information required for an appeal; Chapter Five).

Our framing of open justice in this way adopts a more general model of accountability, where openness and transparency are used to ensure governments or other powerful institutions are answerable and held responsible for their decisions (see Woods et al 2021). In our specific context, 'open justice' describes the application of provisions for openness and transparency in the justice system that ensures the judiciary, the Executive and other decision-making actors are held to account for the way in which justice is delivered. It should be noted, however, that 'transparency' is used metaphorically to explain sharing information and events with the public, and we need to be attuned to varying uses of the term. Further, transparency initiatives may be restricted in some way, and do not necessarily lead to 'information open to all' (Woods et al 2021, p 580).[8]

Also drawing on more general models of accountability, we contend that public participation is essential as part of the accountability process. Models of public participation in systems of governance operate to assist with accountability. In fact, there exists 'general agreement that participatory institutions are a necessary condition for accountability, especially where top-down institutions are malfunctioning or missing' (Barr et al 2014, p 250). Modes of participatory accountability are, perhaps, more obvious in settings such as healthcare or education systems (see Barr et al 2014; Sang 2004). In such settings, governments might create specific institutions that encourage people to hold state agencies to account for their actions and decision-making processes through public policy procedures (Speer 2012). In these institutions, the public might benefit from the active engagement of a few people who join participatory accountability models (Barr et al 2014). The importance with which developmental organisations regard participatory accountability as a mode of governance is illustrated by evidence indicating that such practices 'are implemented in a large number of developing countries and they are firmly anchored in the reform advice strategies of most donors and development non-governmental organizations' (Speer 2012, p 2379).

In such systems, participatory accountability 'improves public service delivery, […] it empowers citizens and […] it deepens democracy', including by increasing the responsiveness of governmental organisations to citizen concerns (Speer 2012, p 2379). While the evidence for using participatory accountability as a mode of governance in the development context is mixed (Speer 2012), it seems to us that there is considerable relevance of such an approach for our discussion of public accountability of the justice system. We perceive an overlap between a model of participatory accountability as a system of governance and the model of open justice which encourages public involvement. As such, we view open justice as a way of facilitating participatory accountability in the justice system.

Our work is informed by a model of 'justice reporting' offered by Chamberlain et al (2021) that looked beyond 'news values' (criteria that influence editorial decisions and priorities) to consider what wider accountability purposes court reporting might serve. Additionally, we adopt Susskind's (2019) description of 'information transparency' as essential as 'real-time observation' of the courts in delivering open justice. Although we do not attempt to mount a developed doctrinal argument in this book, which is firmly focused on policy and practice, it must be noted that the principle of open justice straddles various areas of law. It is understood as a core common law principle essential to the rule of law (Bingham 2006); and integral to the application of Articles 6, 8 and 10 of the European Convention on Human Rights, which protect, respectively the right to a fair and public hearing, the right to a private and family life, and the right to freedom of expression (including the right to receive as well as impart information).[9]

Methods

This book draws on many interdisciplinary sources to provide support for the analysis and argument. Our intention is not to duplicate the many excellent doctrinal accounts of open justice and accountability that exist (several referenced here). Rather we set out to provide a socio-legal discussion, grounded in the practical detail of court practice and policy. We draw together studies by academics, third sector organisations and governmental and parliamentary evaluations. We also draw on our experiences as researchers in the fields of legal practice and journalism. Additionally, we draw on our own empirical data, including preliminary research undertaken by one of us (Townend) on the impact that data sharing has on offenders and whether this can be justified under the open justice principle; and a project engaging students to conduct courtroom observation studies, briefly outlined now.

Following Chamberlain et al's (2021) lead in Bristol, we conducted a similar study to gather information about open justice as it operated in Magistrates' courts in South East England. In January 2020, we recruited final year law students to conduct courtroom observations: to experience and monitor the practice of court reporting and record the types of issues that were raised in cases. This included assessing the 'newsworthiness' of cases as well as factors that might indicate broader systemic issues in the criminal justice system. During March 2020, the students observed 43 cases in a local Magistrates' court. Ongoing observation was stymied by the COVID-19 pandemic and lockdown measures imposed later that month. We tried, unsuccessfully, to gain access to information about court hearings as researchers (see Chapter Three). Recognising the limitations of the dataset, we repeated the study with different students in spring 2022. In total, we gathered data on 83 cases.[10]

We conducted thematic analysis (Braun and Clarke 2022) of that data and of notes made during debriefing sessions with the students. The observations from the study inform and supplement the secondary data presented throughout the book. Like Chamberlain et al (2021), we can provide no more than a snapshot in the location studied. Nonetheless, the data that we obtained showed parallels with the Bristol study, and with other reports and sources of information about how open justice tends to operate in contemporary criminal proceedings. While we do not make claims about broad generalisability, and all references to our study should be read in that context, we suggest that it adds supporting evidence about the limitations of open justice practices. The weight of the information available indicates it is time to re-evaluate how open justice should operate in contemporary society.

Structure of the book

We progress this work by analysing, in our next chapter, methods of accountability of criminal court proceedings, including the principle of open justice. In doing so, we analyse which aspects of open justice are most relevant in Magistrates' courts and examine how these have been given effect historically and their relationship with the ideology that shapes administration of justice in Magistrates' courts. Here we contend that various ideological and practical factors combine to limit the extent to which open justice is delivered.

Chapter Three then considers the operationalisation of open justice in the context of modernisation, digitalisation and data developments in the courts. It is argued that greater reliance on technology in criminal proceedings not only damages the ability of people (whether they are parties to proceedings or not) to participate in the court process, but also undermines accountability and transparency, with negative implications for legitimacy and public legal education.

In Chapter Four we turn to the role and interests of the public and the news media in observing and reporting court. As well as attending to the practical detail of their work (which is often overlooked in policy and judicial discussions), we unpack the rationales justifying their presence in court, and begin to develop our conceptualisation of open justice that goes beyond the news media. In doing so, we consider factors of 'justice-worthiness' as well as the 'newsworthiness' of cases in court. We also show how systemic failures are often mechanical rather than legal faults.

The obvious next step, in Chapter Five, is to consider the 'human impact' of both the rules and the operationalisation of open justice in practice. This, we contend, has been severely neglected in policy and judicial exercises, with assumptions often made about the effects of publicity (even in the face of countervailing evidence). Though we cannot offer full answers based on our preliminary research (and, indeed, some tensions can never be ironed out), we propose that systems should be designed to maximise equal and fair outcomes, and minimise unnecessary stigmatisation and intrusion on individuals to avoid further entrenching existing societal exclusion and inequalities.

Finally, we conclude by arguing for a broad approach to open justice that recognises the importance of public participation in a model of justice system accountability and does not wholly rely on the news media as a proxy for transparency. We offer recommendations for implementing more nuanced and evidence-based approaches to open justice that respond to advances in digital technologies and, in doing so, also attempt to lessen systemic and individualistic harms, including stigmatisation.

Notes

1 Cited in *Scott v Scott* [1913] AC 407, 477.

2 Focus group participant, 2018. For details of the research conducted by Townend, see Chapter Five.

3 To which one of us (Townend) gave oral and written evidence.

4 For a fuller analysis of the committee's recommendations see Townend (2023).

5 When we refer to the media or the 'news media' we are referring to broadcasters, national and local newspapers, and news magazines (and their online publications), which are increasingly also referred to as the 'accredited' media; a problematic category as discussed in Chapter Four. When we refer to the wider online and social media we are thinking of a broader category of publishers that includes members of the public writing on social media platforms and blogs, as well as those operating professionally (as journalists, academics, and justice campaigners – for example).

6 Both within and outside the UK; one of the authors has previously conducted research on 'justice system data' in the UK, Ireland, Canada and Australia (Townend 2019; Townend and Wiener 2021).

7 *Attorney General v Leveller Magazine Ltd* [1979] AC 440; *A v British Broadcasting Corporation* [2014] UKSC 25; *R (on the application of C) v Secretary of State for Justice* [2016] UKSC 2; *Khuja (formerly PNM) v Times Newspapers Limited* [2017] UKSC 49.

8 It is not our ambition in this short policy title to fully dissect varying models for accountability, oversight and transparency. However, these terms should be assessed critically. On the potential obscuring role of metaphors and tropes in the context of freedom of expression, we are guided by Haig Bosmajian (1992). For in-depth critical accounts of transparency and accountability models and terminology, see Fox (2010) and Koivisto (2022).

9. For an overview of open justice in English law, see Rowbottom (2018), pp 129–156.
10. For reasons of space, we have not included a detailed description of our methods here. Further information available from the authors on request. The research was granted University ethical approval under references ER/LCW29/3 and ER/LCW29/5.

TWO

A History of Accountability in Criminal Courts

Introduction

This chapter provides historical context on the way in which open justice and accountability have developed in England and Wales. It considers modes of accountability in the criminal process, public participation in the criminal courts, and its development in recent decades. We consider the place of open justice in a wider tradition of justice system accountability, sitting alongside and underpinning other important tools, such as inspectorates, complaints mechanisms, rights of appeal, post appeal reviews and judicial review. As part of this exercise, we detail the main methods for contemporary observation of physical criminal court hearings and access to different information types.

We also explore the main theoretical rationales for the contemporary approach to open justice – as articulated variously by practitioners, scholars, and judges – which can be categorised, we suggest, as punitive (shaming), deterring, educational, scrutable (ensuring fairness and proper conduct). The chapter then critiques these various arguments, proposing that understandings of justice system accountability need to recognise the distinction in the rationales, and their weaknesses and strengths. We introduce one of our core arguments, that policy and law makers should prioritise informational transparency as a means of scrutiny and education, rather than as a means of an individual's punishment and deterrence.

Accountability and access to justice in the criminal process

Although often conflated with the ability of people to access legal representation, access to justice is a broad and multifaceted concept. Emerging in the 1970s as a social right (Cappelletti et al 1976), access to justice has come to encompass issues such as complexity in application procedures (Adams-Prassl and Adams-Prassl 2020), intellectual, practical, emotional, and attitudinal barriers (McKeever et al 2022), and the ability to understand and participate in proceedings (Welsh 2022), in addition to the ability to access specialised legal advice (Cornford 2016). Byrom offers an 'irreducible minimum standard' of access to justice 'composed of the following elements: (i) access to the formal legal system, (ii) access to an effective hearing, (iii) access to a decision in accordance with substantive law, (iv) access to remedy' (2019, p 4). Emerging from these understandings of access to justice are multiple principles that people may need to invoke to vindicate their legal rights in any circumstance. Participation is key to invoking legal rights, and meaningful participation cannot happen unless participants are able to understand the legal process (McKeever et al 2022; Welsh 2022). It is only once people fully understand the legal process that they can begin to hold it accountable. Public legal education is, therefore, critical to achieving access to justice and accountability.

Accountability is, of itself, essential to achieving access to justice: it enables people to vindicate their rights (see Cornford 2016). As we discuss further throughout this book, accountability can be achieved in two ways; through formal methods that challenge decision-making and outcomes, and through public engagement throughout the process of administering justice. According to Chan (1999), accountability is the obligation to explain, and justify, behaviour. It may also be forward-looking to prevent future failings (Welsh et al 2021). A miserable but helpful illustration of accountability mechanisms is provided in the tragically long running aftermath of the Hillsborough disaster (as a result of which 97 people lost their lives, and over 760 people were injured at a football match). Several methods, including judicial inquiries, police complaints processes, criminal investigations, civil litigation, Coroners' inquests, appeals processes, judicial review (though not granted), private prosecutions and an Independent Panel, were used to hold various organisations to account for the disaster (Welsh et al 2021, p 519). The media, and campaigns by the Hillsborough Family Support Group, also demonstrated the important role that the public can play in challenging criminal process failings. That people are able to hold agencies of the criminal process to account is fundamental in enabling citizens to trust the processes thorough which the state exercises power (Tyler and Huo 2002).

Diverse accountability mechanisms exist in criminal justice. Accountability in the form of monitoring and regulation, as well as ex post facto accountability may be performed by agencies including democratically elected Police and Crime Commissioners, voluntary and third sector campaign organisations, Royal Commissions, complaints departments (within, for example the Crown Prosecution Service), and inspectorates (for example, HM Prison Inspectorate), and the post-appeal review body, the Criminal Cases Review Commission.[1] Decision-making by the police, the Crown Prosecution Service, both Magistrates' and Crown Courts can also be held accountable by the High Court through judicial review in accordance with Part 54.4 Civil Procedure Rules, although this is to be considered to be a remedy of last resort.[2]

How, then, does one achieve accountability of the justice process in the criminal courts? Criminal courts themselves are places where the actions of state agencies may be held to account (Craig 2019; Owusu-Bempah 2016; Ho 2008). The criminal trial process has evolved ways to deal with inappropriate police, prosecution, or defence behaviour. Not only are courts expected to uphold the principles that underpin the right to a fair trial enshrined in Article 6

European Convention on Human Rights (ECHR), but judges are afforded a significant amount of discretion (under the Police and Criminal Evidence Act 1984 (PACE)) about what to do with evidence that may have been obtained unfairly. Additionally, magistrates and judges are expected to hold the parties to certain behavioural standards by actively managing the court process and ensuring compliance with the Criminal Procedure Rules (Crim PR). The criminal process is thus formally highly regulated to uphold the integrity of the system and make it publicly accountable through one arm of the state: the judiciary.

As these accountability mechanisms rely heavily on discretionary decision making, it is likely that regulations and rules will be implemented according to the needs of certain groups or priorities. This can result in an operational gap, whereby 'implementation is often dependent on the joint actions of large numbers of semi-autonomous actors, each having their own interests, agendas and views, that may or may not be in line with the policy mandate' (Terpstra and Fyfe 2015, p 540). Among others, Young (2013) and Welsh (2022) explained how the courtroom 'workgroup'[3] may adapt to various forms of intervention by invoking principles of organisational culture. Thus, organisational approaches to implementation of policy and regulatory mechanisms may frustrate the purpose of formal rules. As the agencies of criminal justice are generally self-regulating and are largely dependent on the application of professional discretion, wrongdoing may be difficult to effectively challenge (Welsh et al 2021). We suggest, then, that independent mechanisms of accountability are required to ensure the integrity of the criminal process. Those mechanisms include engaging the public through inquiries, the ability of the public to observe the criminal courts, and independent academic scrutiny.

Regarding the latter, academics may produce qualitative and/or quantitative data about the criminal process, but also make use of government-produced statistics such as the

Ministry of Justice's *Criminal Justice Statistics Quarterly* bulletins and associated overview tables.[4] Criminal Justice Statistics Quarterly produces quantitative data about case progression and outcomes, while reports on first time entrants to the criminal justice system and re-offending rates has recently been added to the Ministry of Justice datasets. However, much published data is fragmented and paints an incomplete picture. It is necessary, then, for academics to seek direct access to additional data at source. Since court and tribunal records are largely exempt from the Freedom of Information Act 2000,[5] with access also limited under the Environmental Information Regulations 2004, permission for access to unpublished court records must be sought directly from the data owners or requested directly from the courts under the Crim PR and Crim PD.

In mid-2020, the Ministry of Justice announced its Data First initiative that links administrative datasets from across the justice system, 'enabling accredited researchers, across government and academia, to access anonymised, research-ready datasets ethically and responsibly' (Ministry of Justice 2022a, p 4). An application to access a dataset compiled via Data First will be assessed against criteria including: the data owner's areas of research interest; the overall benefit to the data owner and wider public; resources required to fulfil the request as well as consideration of ethics and data protection and security. Applications by researchers applying to the HM Courts and Tribunals Service (HMCTS) Data Access Panel (DAP) (for court datasets outside the Data First scheme) will be assessed against the same criteria (HMCTS 2023d). In this way, only if proposed research sits within the parameters of the data owners' areas of interest will access be granted. Furthermore, access will only be granted if provision does not place – in the data holder's view – too much strain on its resources.

Even where court records are deemed public, and therefore do not require special permission for access via the Data First process or DAP, there may be issues using such records for the purpose of research because of the way in which files are stored, formatted or because of the high costs involved in obtaining them (Townend 2013; Byrom 2019). Additionally, researchers who wish to conduct interviews with members of the judiciary are asked to approach the Judicial Office. Access to much court related data is thus restricted by gatekeepers, which may stifle the extent to which evaluative academic research can examine issues of accountability and transparency. This highlights the importance of open justice (whereby courts can be monitored without special permission), as an enabler of research that enhances public understanding and accountability of the justice system.

Ultimately, accountability mechanisms are plentiful but imperfect. Resources are stretched, discretion – while important to avoid rigidity that may not match individual case needs – may lead to inconsistency, arbitrariness, or (at worst) corruption. In recognition of the need for the criminal process to inspire public confidence, there is a long history of public engagement in criminal justice through an approach of openness and transparency.

Theoretical rationales underpinning open criminal justice

Holding trials in public places is part of state accountability and promotes inclusivity in court proceedings. The public's ability to scrutinise the role and behaviour of the state is particularly crucial in the criminal context. Whereas in the civil justice system, complainants and defendants usually appear as private citizens (with some exceptions[6]), in criminal proceedings, the state almost invariably takes over the case from the complainant or victim and progresses it through the judicial system (Welsh et al 2021). Further, the state imposes punishment, and has the ability to legitimately interfere with someone's right to liberty (Article 5 ECHR). In light of these wide-ranging state powers, the criminal process is public facing, and needs to remain so to retain legitimacy. As Shnoor and Katvan (2019) argued in the

Israeli context, transparency in the criminal process is key to public understanding and trust, even if it undermines the 'perfect façade' of an objective, independent and untainted judiciary.[7]

An important related element of criminal law and process lies in its declaratory function. As Ashworth and Horder said:

> To criminalize a certain kind of conduct is to declare that it is a public wrong that should not be done, to institute a threat of punishment in order to supply a pragmatic reason for not doing it, and to censure those who nevertheless do it. (2013, p 22)

For our purposes, the key to this assertion lies in the public nature of criminal law and the process of denouncing those who are convicted of violating it. Indeed, eminent criminal law scholars have in common that a key element of criminalisation lies in declaring *public* wrongs before imposing socially legitimated punishment (Duff 2014; Edwards and Simester 2017). The criminal trial is, therefore, a place where the structural violence of the criminal process and potential for punishment is publicly inflicted on the defendant (Leader 2021) in furtherance of the authority of the state.

But there are also wider functions for the criminal law and process: an educational function that publicly demonstrates which behaviour is considered unacceptable, allows people to understand how the law operates (Mulcahy and Rowden 2019) and offers an opportunity to identify wrongful applications of law; a shaming function (in relation to the recipient of punishment); and a censuring function (public expressions of disapproval). It was through *performing* punishment that 'community justice and official sanction became most closely intertwined' through public parades to pillories, or processions of punishment (Banks 2014, p 24). However, public shaming of this nature steadily declined in the 19th and 20th centuries, as public space was reformed, and imprisonment became a more commonly imposed method of punishment (Banks 2014).

One key aim of punishment is deterrence, which is both individual (to the offender) and general (to wider society). Eighteenth century legal philosophers argued that the constructive purpose of *publicly* punishing people was crime prevention through deterrence and shaming (Nagin 2013). Historically, inflicting punishment for crime in public attracted spectators, especially if the punishment was cruel (Bruinsma 2018; Garvey 1998). Indeed, '[s]hame involves the *idea* of an audience' (Garvey 1998, p 766, original emphasis). Garvey views media reporting of sentencing as a way of 'heap[ing] ignominy' on offenders through modern methods of communication (1998, p 737). Publicly communicating punishment and law enforcement policies may work as a way of nudging people away from criminal activity (Pickett 2018) in a 'politically viable and cost-effective way of achieving deterrence' (Garvey 1998, p 738). On shaming, see further Chapter Five.

The evidence of deterrent effects of publicity is, however, debatable. While there is some evidence that deterrence works (for example, Khadjavi 2018), 'studies of the relationship between the volume of news coverage of crime and actual rates of crime find the relationship to be close to non-existent' (Kleck et al 2005, p 630). The ability of communicating outcomes to deter people from crime is not well studied (Pickett 2018). Further, many deterrence-based arguments for publicity are 'highly speculative' (Kahan 2006, p 2089; see also Hart 2014; Fitz-gibbon and O'Brien 2017).

Shaming for both individual and general deterrent purposes might theoretically appeal to those imposing punishment, but punishment does not of itself require publicity, and Hadjimatheou (2016) argued that it has yet to be demonstrated that labelling criminals reduces first-time offending more than it aggravates recidivism. On the contrary, and regardless of the actual sentence imposed, to publicly label a person's behaviour as criminal might have such a stigmatising effect that the person may be pushed further towards deviant subcultures and recidivism (Hopkins Burke

2014; Ugwudike 2015), even at an intergenerational level (Besemer et al 2017).

There are, criminologists have observed, power differentials involved in labelling a person's behaviour as criminal, and an increasing tendency to stigmatise behaviour though the criminal justice process (Hopkins Burke 2014). This body of work on 'labelling theory' indicates that individual deterrence through publicly shaming defendants is unlikely to be successful in reducing reoffending; and the impact on general deterrence is unclear.

Despite these analyses, important questions remain about whether publicity in relation to criminal sanctions is required 'for transparency and openness in criminal justice; the right of people to know about the criminality of others; the need to reduce the risk posed by ex-offenders to the public; or the potential reassurance publicity might offer the public' (Hadjimatheou 2016, p 570). If we seek to meaningfully exercise the educational and deterrent principles of criminal law and procedure, we must move beyond focussing only on punishment, and ensure that public engagement with the whole criminal process is fairly and accurately reported. In this book, we suggest a shift in emphasis, moving away from an account of publicity in criminal proceedings as important for shaming and/or deterrence purposes, to one that considers the broader importance of making the justice system scrutable and of its educational value in the widest sense.

The deterrence and labelling arguments highlight the educative and shaming functions of the public criminal process (however damaging the effects). We now turn our attention to the way that this publicity enables the state to be held accountable by the judiciary and lay participants in the process (juries and magistrates).

Publicly holding state agencies to account

As noted previously, courts have significant powers to hold the agencies of criminal justice to account during proceedings themselves. The Crim PR and Crim PD, which govern the behaviour of participants, state the rules that parties must follow during the prosecution of a suspected crime, including the overriding objective that cases be dealt with 'justly' (Crim PR 1.1). Dealing with cases justly includes a number of factors, including acquitting the innocent and convicting the guilty; treating participants with politeness and respect; dealing with the parties fairly; recognising the rights of a defendant, including those under Article 6 ECHR; dealing with the case efficiently and expeditiously. Courts are required to actively manage the duties of the parties to ensure that they meet the aims of the Crim PR, and the principle of open justice is reflected in Crim PR 5.7, which states:

> the court officer and the court must have regard to the importance of– (a) dealing with criminal cases in public; (b) allowing a public hearing to be reported to the public; and (c) the rights of a person affected by a direction or order made, or warrant issued, by the court to understand why that decision was made.

Crim PR 5.8 explains how courts must deal with requests for information from the public or media reporters, making clear that courts should provide information about cases provided that (among other requirements about notification) there are no reporting restrictions on the matter, the trial verdict was delivered less than six months ago, and the information is readily available to the court officer. Although these rules apply to the public, HMCTS guidance and the Crim PD 2023 (and previous versions) prioritise access by 'accredited' journalists over the wider public, as we consider in more detail in Chapter Four.

Accountability of the parties is arguably implicit in many of these rules and bolstered by statute or case law in particularly challenging areas. It is clear from these principles that accountability is considered important across the whole process, meaning that to focus on sentencing or trials (in fact rare in the criminal process) ignores that allowing open justice in relation to courts generally is a vital tool for evaluating the system holistically. It is a mistake, as Bandes and Feigenson (2020) argued, to focus on open justice only in relation to the main event of a trial and ignore the backstage work that occurs before the trial takes place.

Accountability of this nature is performed publicly in both Magistrates' and Crown Courts. Judicial office holders in both the Magistrates' and Crown Courts are empowered to exclude evidence when its admission would have such an adverse effect on the fairness of proceedings that the court ought not admit it (s.78 PACE). Such exclusionary rules might reflect the modern conception of the criminal trial as about protecting people from inappropriate use of state power (Ho 2008). Applications to exclude evidence may be made alongside submissions that admitting evidence would breach the defendant's right to a fair trial under Article 6 ECHR, or abuses of state power (such as under s.76(2) PACE, governing improperly obtained confessions, or provisions regarding breaches of police powers in relation to covert surveillance), or circumstances in which the integrity of the criminal process would be brought into disrepute such that the proceedings amount to an affront to public justice.[8] The courts have a residual discretion to exclude evidence where its probative value is outweighed by the prejudicial effect of admitting the evidence.[9] Additionally, under s.19 and s.19A Prosecution of Offences Act 1985, the courts can make a wasted costs order against a party where there has been an improper or unnecessary act or omission, and that act or omission has caused costs to be incurred. Each of these ways of holding state agencies accountable in the criminal process is conducted publicly in adult criminal courts. Legal arguments about the admissibility of evidence as a result of impropriety are conducted in open court, where members of the public are entitled to sit in the gallery and observe the arguments, the judicial ruling, and make notes about the same if they so choose. As Bosland and Gill stated, open justice requires that, usually,

> judicial proceedings are conducted, and decisions pronounced, in 'open court'; second, that evidence is communicated publicly to those present in the court; and, third, that nothing should be done to discourage the making of fair and accurate reports of judicial proceedings, including by the media. (2015, pp 483–484)

These judicial obligations encourage accountability, but also allow members of the public to develop their understanding of the criminal law and process and serve the declaratory function of criminal process (given previously). These obligations offer significant constitutional checks.[10]

As Colbran (2003) argued, open justice can also assist (albeit imperfectly) with encouraging accountability in judicial decision-making too. Historically, public observers of court proceedings have been regarded as not only spectators in proceedings, but also as 'regulators of the behaviour of judges, able to complain when the judge appeared impartial or lacking in independence' (Mulcahy and Rowden 2019, p 7). Additionally, when even a few citizens observe a trial process and believe it to be conducted unfairly, it raises the possibility of both the law and public officials facing criticism, with the potential to extend debate beyond the courtroom itself and promote change (Ferguson 2007). Public access to court proceedings is thus an 'essential check and balance' on judicial power (Bandes and Feigenson 2020, p 1334). One Lord Chief Justice recognised that open justice could deter improper court behaviour, while also enabling the public to know that judicial work is conducted impartially (Justice Committee 2022a). There are, however, exceptions to open justice when proceedings can be held privately (*in camera*). *In camera* proceedings may be appropriate where the administration of justice could be affected by prejudicial information made available publicly (such as public interest immunity (PII) hearings where the prosecution seek to withhold sensitive information from disclosure), or to prevent other harm such as to a young person or victim of a sexual offence (Bosland and Gill 2015).

Importantly, public access is presumed as 'an indispensable attribute of the Anglo-American legal system' (Matenaer 2021, p 694), and the principle of public justice is enshrined in the ECHR. Nonetheless, the principles on which public justice is based are seldom debated in case law or commentary on the criminal process (Duff et al 2007). Two ends of a spectrum appear to emerge. On the one hand, open justice in criminal courts exists to hold *the state* to account for the way it treats defendants and citizens (Ho 2008; Owusu-Bempah 2016; Craig 2019). To Craig, the 'principle of open justice is designed to be deployed *against* those in power' (2019, p 140, original emphasis), and the right to a fair and public hearing is that of the defendant and not of the general public. Craig (2019) is right that there is a difference between disseminating general trial information and disseminating details of a person's identity; and dissemination of more than generic trial information may be explained by the modern tendency to try and nudge behaviour through naming and shaming 'undeserving' criminals (Welsh 2022). Our concern is that a focus on naming and shaming might obscure the significance of other functions of open justice, especially in the current climate which has impeded the ability of lawyers to operate as a check on judicial power in light of legal aid cuts (Welsh 2022).

On the other hand, criminal trials exist to call defendants to account in relation to the charges: 'the trial is a communicative forum which involves mutual relations of responsibility between the parties' (Duff et al 2007, p 3). As such, there is also a communicative element to the criminal trial in holding defendants accountable their actions. In their analysis, Duff et al (2007) believed that the best rationale for publicly conducted trials is that they 'allow critical public scrutiny of the participatory processes of the trial' (2007, p 4), while – at the same time – '[t]rials and punishments, it is argued, are [...] aimed at, or at least bring about, the social exclusion of offenders in response to a vindicative retributive impulse' (2007, p 3).

We can see, then, that the aims of criminal law, procedure, and punishment – all of which make up the criminal process – reflect needs for both public and individual censure (and, therefore, education), and a need to hold the state to account. As a general theory of criminal trials has not yet been developed (Duff et al 2007), we do not, here, feel that it is necessary for open justice to be placed at either end of the individual versus state accountability spectrum. Ho advocates for moderate views, acknowledging that a trial may be about a search for the truth in a particular case, but it also has subsidiary rule of law aims in which 'the criminal trial should be construed *essentially* as a process of *calling the state to account for its request for condemnation and punishment*' (2008 p 4, original emphasis). We regard both individual and state accountability through the criminal process and open justice as important, especially when analysis moves beyond the trial process itself. Overlaps and tension may exist between the purposes of criminal law (which are communicative, declaring public wrongs) and purposes of criminal process and rules of evidence (holding both state and defendant to account in the administration of law), but without open justice it would be difficult to observe whether any of these aims are being met.

We suggest that the basis upon which magistrates and judges may exercise their powers as a method of regulating and holding criminal justice agencies to account is grounded in four broad principles: ensuring that the case is decided only on reliable evidence; disciplining state agencies who may have misused or abused their powers; preserving the moral integrity of the system and thereby improving public confidence; and protecting defendants from unfairly obtained prosecutorial advantage (see Welsh et al 2021). That all stages of the judiciary can exercise such powers is of fundamental importance in holding the justice system to account, and the fact that it operates in publicly accessible courts should help increase confidence in the justice system overall, as well as educating citizens about their rights and the duties of the state in matters of criminal process. We are of the view that systematic observation of criminal courts by the media, but also by researchers and the public, can uncover issues relevant to accountability, and encourage debate in these areas.

Public participation in criminal courts

The entirety of the criminal process in England and Wales relies on public engagement and cooperation. The most obvious example of this is through victim and witness engagement with the police, without whom a significant proportion of crime would go undetected, let alone prosecuted and punished. Indeed, examinations of the justice gap in relation to hate crime (Walters et al 2017), and attrition rates in relation to domestic abuse and sexual offence cases (Temkin and Krahé 2008), highlight how important it is for the criminal process to be accessible and engage meaningfully with the public. Thus, for many decades, the consent of the community has been regarded as key not only to trust and confidence in policing, but also to effective policing on the understanding that 'the police are dependent on public support in reporting crime and assisting with criminal justice outcomes' (Torrible 2022, p 171).

How, then, at trial stage are members of the public involved? Defendants are effectively compelled to participate in the criminal justice process given the powers of arrest and detention that the police and courts can exercise (Owusu-Bempah 2016). However, the participation of other members of the public is essential to the functioning of the system. If a suspect is charged with a criminal offence, prosecuting authorities then also become reliant on maintaining good relationships with victims and witnesses, without whose continued cooperation many prosecutions would simply fail for lack of evidence (McGuire et al 2021). While prosecuting authorities and courts have powers to compel the public to participate in the criminal process as witnesses, the decision to effectively force a reluctant member of the public to (continue to) participate in the criminal process is not a straightforward one. In her study of domestic abuse cases, Porter (2019) found that although prosecutors often invoked the power to summons a reluctant witness (instead of implementing powers to read an absent witness's statement in ss.114–116 Criminal Justice Act 2003), they were aware that forcing people to participate in the process was not a decision to be taken lightly. We can see, then, that the criminal process as we know it would largely cease to function if the public did not willingly participate in it.

Processes of both adjudication and sentencing also depend on public participation. In the Crown Court, this is most obviously recognisable through the participation of members of juries in deciding whether a defendant is guilty of an offence. In England and Wales, juries are specifically recognised as having a lay role only to decide whether a defendant is guilty or not; they do not decide matters of evidential admissibility, and do not play a role in sentencing. Juries do, however, decide whether a defendant's actions warrant punishment at all.

Juries almost always consist of 12 members of the public (this can be reduced in certain circumstances) who have been randomly selected for jury service based on their entry on the electoral roll (s.3 Juries Act 1974). While there are a number of exceptions to eligibility for, and disqualifications from, jury service, it is broadly regarded as a civic duty in which those who are summonsed should participate. Evidence suggests that jury service does increase participants' sense of pride while also leading to better understanding of, and more interest in, the administration of justice overall (Matthews et al 2004). Thus, one important value of jury service is in increasing public understanding about, and engagement with, the criminal process. It is only with such understanding that the system is capable of being accountable to the community that it serves.

Community (albeit a contested concept; see Crow and Mah 2012) is another significant value in lay participation in criminal justice. Public participation in proceedings 'serves as a powerful reminder that the proceedings are not merely a private interchange, but a function performed on behalf of the community, in which community-wide problems are addressed and norms articulated' (Bandes and Feigenson 2020, p 1333). Juries represent a democratic function, occupying a position as lay public participants in the interpretation and administration of legal process. As Carroll argued, 'jurors become a source of law as they contemplate the defendant's fate, mapping the law across their own lives in the process' (2014, p 827).

A rationale for trial by jury is that the defendant's conduct is 'assessed according to local norms by twelve ordinary people whose outlooks have been moulded by their diverse characters, histories and life styles' (Daly and Pattenden, 2005, p 681). While the representative nature of juries in England and Wales is contested, with Thomas and Balmer finding that 'jurors were remarkably representative of the local community in terms of: ethnicity, gender, income, occupation, religion and age (except 65–69 years olds [sic])' (2007, p iii), the importance of underpinning themes of community engagement, public participation in the criminal process, and democratic accountability should not be lost in concerns about the composition of juries themselves. In fact, perceptions that juries are not representative (Jacobson et al 2015) should increase our efforts to improve the accountability and openness of proceedings.

This section has shown how public engagement is critical to the criminal process at all levels. This is key, we have said, to maintaining public confidence in the courts. While we are committed to this agenda, we should note that research on whether direct contact with the criminal justice process improves confidence in the system is mixed (see, for example,

Van de Walle 2009; Marsh et al 2019). A perverse effect of greater transparency and direct experience is that failings might be observed, and therefore lower public confidence. This is something we return to in Chapter Five when considering the human impacts of transparency policy; ultimately, we find that any negative impact on public confidence must be embraced as part of the accountability process, and ideally, will lead to longer term improvements. We now consider the Magistrates' courts, as a focal example to our discussion, to consider how public participation is achieved in this setting.

Public participation in Magistrates' courts

King Edward I first commissioned 'good and lawful men' to keep the peace in designated counties, representing an early iteration of the concept of localised justice, and in 1361, the Justice of the Peace Act formalised the early role of the magistracy. The nature and accessibility of early summary justice appears to have differed depending on whether proceedings were conducted in urban or rural areas. In rural areas, magistrates 'sat in their parlours or in local inns' (Gray 2008, p 8). However, in the 18th century, summary justice was, according to McBarnet (1981), conducted privately behind closed doors, and this was objected to. Suspicion had grown about the propriety of citizens being 'imprisoned merely at the discretion of a magistrate', especially as many people were imprisoned without a formal summary trial during this period (Dabhoiwala 2006, p 797). It seems that efforts to engage the wider public increased from this time.

By the late 18th century, in an early effort to engage the public in the administration of justice in Magistrates' courts, magistrate and social reformer Sir John Fielding regularly opened what was to become Bow Street Magistrates' Court to the public to allow 'a large audience for his examinations of suspected offenders'; this would 'strengthen the prosecution process by engaging the public interest and encouraging victims of crime not only to report offences, but to attend [...] in the hope that they would be able to identify their assailants and so be able to add their evidence to prosecution cases' (Beattie 2007, p 71). Fielding's efforts to engage the public were successful: 'The new courtroom had seats for the public who were encouraged to come if they thought they might recognize some of the defendants or simply out of interest. Bow Street was frequently crowded on these occasions' (Beattie 2007, p 85). Several other magistrates' offices were established in public places as opposed to private houses where magistrates had previously sat. Fielding advertised the opening hours of the offices to encourage public attendance (Beattie 2007). By 1800, there was a continuous system of summary justice that took place at well-defined, regular times in public spaces, according to Gray (2008). These early Magistrates' courts were established in ways 'that most or many people could use and it is evident that Londoners were using them in considerable numbers' (Gray 2008, p 14). However, such pre-trial public engagement was not universally supported amid fears that it may prejudice a jury later hearing the case. Those objections led many newspapers of the era to stop or limit their publication of what happened at Bow Street in particular (Beattie 2007).

As professional police forces developed in the 1800s, the first appointed employed magistrates – stipendiaries – were introduced following the Municipal Corporations Act 1835. Magistrates and stipendiaries (now District Judges) continued to implement local criminal justice in courts of Petty Sessions until the Magistrates' courts were formally created in 1971. Today, local advisory committees consisting of both magistrates and non-magistrates appoint people who have applied and been selected as meeting the attributes required to become a magistrate (Magistrates' Association, no date). Magistrates are trained, but do not need to be legally qualified to sit in court. Magistrates must sit for a minimum of 26 half days per year, for which they are unpaid (but can claim some expenses). A qualified court legal adviser sits with magistrates to ensure the legality of their decision making but plays no role in their determinations on the facts of cases.

In this way, magistrates preside over cases as lay members of the judiciary. Magistrates share the jury's role as sole arbiter of facts, but also share judicial functions in the passing of sentences and making of orders. Sometimes, legally qualified District Judges sit in Magistrates' courts, where they can exercise both the functions of judge and jury. Magistrates hear pleas in summary offences (those which carry a maximum sentence of six months imprisonment), and in either way offences (those which can be dealt with either by magistrates or by a judge and jury at first instance). Magistrates send indictable only matters (those which are too serious to be dealt with summarily and can only be dealt with by a judge and jury) to the Crown Court to be dealt with. Magistrates may try and sentence summary only offences and either way offences where their sentencing powers are sufficient. For many decades, magistrates' sentencing powers were restricted to six months imprisonment for any number of summary only offences and one either way offence, and 12 months imprisonment for two or more either way offences. In 2022, and in light of the court backlog exacerbated by the advent of the COVID-19 pandemic, magistrates' sentencing powers were extended to allow them to impose a prison sentence of up to 12 months for a single offence (Ministry of Justice 2022b). In March 2023, however, the government confirmed this would be 'temporarily' reduced to six months (per the original approach) citing 'downstream pressures in the criminal justice system'[11] and the need for a 'cohesive cross-system response' in which the Crown Court retains power over decisions in respect of longer sentences (Parliament.uk 2023).

Despite these powers, there is a perception that matters in Magistrates' courts are too trivial to warrant public interest and engagement (McBarnet 1981). In fact, it is the court that members of the public are most likely to come into contact with; all criminal cases begin in Magistrates' courts, around 95 per cent of all criminal cases conclude there. Notwithstanding amendments to sentencing powers, magistrates can impose punishments that significantly impact peoples' lives. Given these factors and the range of case types that magistrates may adjudicate upon, we argue that these courts deserve as much interest as Crown Court proceedings.

In July 2021, there were 12,651 magistrates in England and Wales, representing a significant decline from 25,170 in 2012 (Ministry of Justice 2021b). In December 2021, there were 126 District Judges who sit in Magistrates' courts (Courts and Tribunals Judiciary 2021a). Whatever their iteration, the key strengths of the Magistrates' courts remain their perceived ability to administer local justice, and to be regarded as an 'embodiment of citizen participation in justice' (Donoghue 2014, p 932). For parliament, 'the magistracy's role is traditionally underpinned by the twin principles of "local justice" and "justice by one's peers"' (Justice Committee 2019). The rationale underpinning such appointments is that if a crime is committed, people who know the local communities and issues within them are best placed to decide outcomes (Wilkins 2022).

We can take from these processes that democratic practices and localised accountability have long been considered important features of criminal justice. As Gibson said, '[t]he involvement of ordinary members of the public in the delivery of justice is at the heart of our judicial and social system' (2009, p 19). Democratic accountability through public engagement has become, according to Mulcahy and Rowden, 'something of a truism that, among the many factors contributing to the moral integrity of criminal proceedings, trials are expected to be held in public places in which spectators are able to observe justice being done' (2019, p 7). This, they suggest, operates in principle as a type of 'reverse panopticon in which the many view the few' (2019, p 259). It is to the wider methods of public engagement to which we now turn.

Observing court

It is an oft-quoted fundamental principle of the criminal process that justice should 'not only be done, but should manifestly and undoubtedly be seen to be done'.[12] This extends to public observation of adult criminal court proceedings, except where reporting restrictions have been applied (see Chapter Four). All Magistrates' and Crown Courts in England and Wales should have a seating area (the 'public gallery'), which any member of the public may enter and sit in to observe cases. Although critical of the general public's ability to properly engage in cases from the public galleries, Jaconelli agreed that 'the idea of open justice finds it basic expression in the rule which permits attendance at the trial by members of the public' (2002, p 35). Given the principle of public censure inherent in the criminal process, and the fact that the criminal process operates as an arm of the state, the ability of the public to openly observe what happens in our criminal courts operates as an extension of principles of accountability and democracy in criminal courts of first instance.

The Court of Appeal and UK Supreme Court (UKSC) also have public galleries so that people can attend and see justice being dispensed. Additionally, UKSC proceedings can be live streamed and watched on demand. From 2018, selected civil proceedings in the Court of Appeal were permitted to be live streamed via the judiciary's YouTube channel. While not implemented until 2022, The Crown Court (Recording and Broadcasting) Order 2020 made provision for the recording and broadcasting of judicial sentencing remarks in Crown Courts. The provisions allow media outlets to record and broadcast the judge passing sentence, while other parties to the case will not be visible to protect their privacy. In enabling these provisions to move forward, the Lord Chancellor and Secretary of State for Justice said that filming sentencing of some the country's 'most serious offenders' would 'improve transparency, and reinforce confidence in the justice system. The public will now be able to see justice handed down, helping them understand better the complex decisions judges make' (Ministry of Justice 2022c).

While we would not disagree with encouraging open access to sentencing remarks for the reasons articulated previously, those aims fail to address issues of scrutability during Crown Court proceedings and so are not a panacea to replace the value of in person attendance by media outlets, public observers, researchers and academics who can view the entirety of most proceedings and observe the actual administration of justice (procedural access to justice) rather than only its outcomes (substantive access to justice). The Justice Committee (2022a) suggested that the broadcasting of sentencing remarks could be extended to Magistrates' courts but felt that other elements of criminal trials should not be broadcast.

While legitimate concerns exist about broadcasting the entirety of criminal proceedings (see Moore et al 2021, and, as we see in Chapter Five, even limited publicity may have a detrimental impact on some individuals), making sentencing remarks the most accessible part of the criminal process might undermine the justice system accountability element of open justice, and disproportionately send a message to the public that a) there is little need to attend court in person, and b) the most important part of the criminal process is sentencing.

In the 18th century, a primary aim of encouraging public engagement in hearings was to improve the chances of securing evidence against an accused (Beattie 2007). While this function has essentially fallen away in modern criminal proceedings (Jaconelli 2002), the principle of open justice in criminal proceedings is now deeply embedded in our criminal process to allow parties to a case to observe (after giving any relevant evidence), to allow the media to report, to educate the public about the criminal process, to publicly censure defendants, and – we argue – as a form of participatory accountability.

Following *Ewing v Crown Court Sitting at Cardiff & Newport & Ors*,[13] observers are permitted to take notes of proceedings (unless the court finds it is necessary and proportionate to prohibit note taking).[14] Regular public attendance at court hearings is, however, now uncommon. Although Fielding's courts in the 1700s may have been crowded (Beattie 2007), by the late 1970s, neither press nor the public were frequent attenders at Magistrates' court hearings. McBarnet observed that:

> so rare is it for a member of the public to attend summary courts that the public benches are often used as a waiting room for the morning's batch of defendants, from which they can observe their predecessors' fate and shuffle along to each newly vacated space till their turn comes for the dock. To go to these courts as a member of the public is to become an object of curiosity; to sit there taking notes is to invite paroxysms of paranoia. (1981, p 189)

This trend in Magistrates' courts continued in the 21st century, as 'few citizens see the process with the number of members of the public visiting court having slowly shrunk' (Chamberlain et al 2021, p 2406).[15] Generally, in recent times, 'courtrooms have allocated less and less space to the press and public' (Bandes and Feigenson 2020, p 1346). Mulcahy and Rowden (2019) explained that courtroom design memorandums suggested that restricted sightlines for public observers were considered appropriate, so that observers only have a general view of proceedings. However, a 'public gallery with poor views of principal actors does little to render justice open' (Mulcahy and Rowden 2019, p 241). In their study of Magistrates' courts in Bristol, Chamberlain et al found the public gallery to be 'generally empty except for occasional friends and family of defendants and some witnesses waiting to be called' (2021, p 2412). Student researchers in our own study felt that they were frequently questioned about their presence and felt that such questioning would be unsettling for public observers. The student researchers felt that court staff were unused to seeing observers in court, and that staff became more helpful the more they became familiar with the students, allowing the researchers to gather more information about cases.

That public observation of criminal proceedings invites paranoia from those who administer summary criminal justice or is viewed as 'problematic' (Mulcahy and Rowden 2019, p 265), undermines the notion that the administration of justice should, by default, be conducted publicly (McBarnet 1981). We know, also, that the very presence of courtroom observers can cause professional members of the courtroom to adapt (to try and improve) their behaviour (McCall 1984; Welsh 2022). We know from our own experiences and the accounts of other researchers who have observed Magistrates' courts (Long, forthcoming), that the presence of non-parties to the case invited questions about the reasons for attendance, and sometimes prompted misunderstandings about the rights of observers. In one instance, student researchers were told that they could not write down the names of defendants in cases they observed, even though defendants' names are publicly listed on a noticeboard in the waiting area of the court building, Magistrates' court listings are published online, and no general rule prohibits such practice. The researchers were not offered any explanation for the instruction not to record defendant names.

As outlined by Chamberlain et al, media coverage of the 'judicial system is key to the rule of law and to a democratic society, and independent oversight from journalism is fundamental to the principle of open justice and the notion of journalism as a watchdog on behalf of citizens' (2021, p 2405). Furthermore, journalists have 'played a significant role in uncovering miscarriages of justice in which the judiciary and other state agents have been implicated' (Mulcahy and Rowden 2019, p 8). But as we shall explore in Chapter Four, not only has public attendance at hearings decreased, but media coverage of lower criminal courts has also declined as a nationwide network of court reporters dwindled (Chamberlain et al 2021). Additionally, public confidence in the criminal justice system has declined since the 1980s, attributed to a lack of knowledge and understanding about how the justice system operates (Van de Walle 2009). When public confidence in the criminal process is low, lack of court reporting harms the democratic process (Chamberlain et al 2021). The ability to achieve accountability through public observation is thus undermined when the public and the media are explicitly or implicitly discouraged from observing Magistrates' and other court proceedings. Furthermore, because media reporting of court processes 'appeals to sensationalism through highlighting perceived abuses, incompetence and corruption, not necessarily through thorough evaluation or education' (Colbran 2003, p 57), the ability and motivation of the public (including researchers) to attend hearings is also important for educational and scrutiny purposes. We return to these issues in more depth in Chapter Four.

Before we do so, and despite some cultural shifts towards openness since the 18th century, and the new methods for observing justice in the higher courts, we contend that Magistrates' courts are, in fact, less accessible than they were historically. Just over half of Magistrates' courts closed between 2010 and 2020 (Bowcott and Duncan 2019), and one study of the impact of Magistrates' court closures in Suffolk found that local court closures had reduced the ability of participants and the public to access courts (Adisa 2018). The harder it is to attend a court hearing; the fewer people will engage with the process unless they are compelled to do so. In the next chapter, we will examine how these processes seem to have been made worse because of modernisation and digitalisation, including the introduction of the Single Justice Procedure (SJP) for minor offences, the increased use of virtual courts and the automatic online conviction process.

Summary

This chapter has explained some of the historical context of public engagement in the criminal courts, with particular focus on summary criminal justice. In doing so, public engagement is situated in a narrative of open justice accountability. Without publicly accessible performance of criminal justice, opacity could increase and confidence in the criminal process could dwindle further. Less media scrutiny of summary criminal justice and less public attendance at court potentially perpetuates and entrenches an ideology that Magistrates' courts only deal with trivial matters (McBarnet 1981), which undermines the impact that even a summary criminal conviction may have on an individual, and their family and associates. It also weakens the ability of the criminal process to fulfil its educational function, meaning that public accountability of both the system and of offenders is weakened. We, therefore, argue that informational transparency and participatory accountability need to be prioritised as a means of encouraging justice system scrutability and the educational function of the criminal process.

Notes

1 For detailed discussion, see Welsh et al (2021, ch 11).

2 See, for example, *R(F) v. DPP* [2014] QB 581.

3 Workgroup, in this context, refers to people working in the courts: security staff, ushers, clerks, legal representatives, magistrates and judges.

4 See: https://data.justice.gov.uk/courts and https://www.gov.uk/government/collections/criminal-court-statistics (accessed 4 July 2023).

5 Section 32, Freedom of Information Act (FOIA) 2000; Environmental Information Regulations (EIR) 2004 12(5)(b). Additionally, under the UK General Data Protection Regulation and Data Protection Act 2018, subject access rights do not apply to personal data processed by the judiciary exercising judicial functions. Other types of justice data – relating to the management of courts, for example, may fall outside the FOIA exemption. HMCTS, as an executive agency of the Ministry of Justice (MOJ), is subject to the MOJ publication scheme (MOJ no date).

6 There are some exceptions to this, such as in relation to immigration and asylum claims, some Family court proceedings, or judicial review proceedings, where one party is a state agency.

7 See also Chapter Five, concerning the debate over appropriate use of judicial analytical tools and data.

8 See, for example, *Maxwell* [2011] 1 WLR 1837.

9 *Sang* [1980] AC 402.

10 *Al-Rawi and Ors v. The Security Service and Ors* [2010] EWCA Civ 482.

11 Primarily, overcrowding in male prisons (Magistrates' Association 2023; also see a ministerial response to the Justice Committee 2023).

12 *Sussex Justices, ex parte McCarthy* [1924] 1 KB 256 at 259.

13 [2016] EWHC 183 (Admin).

14 See Crim PD 2.3.

15 We explore this further in Chapter Four.

THREE

Justice System Modernisation, Digitalisation and Data

Introduction

This chapter provides a descriptive analysis of 21st century criminal justice remodelling, including the ways in which digital technology has been adopted in the English and Welsh justice system, and some of the ramifications for digital data dissemination and publication. We will draw out connections between digitalisation and the principle of open justice as the chapter progresses. We focus on aspects of HM Courts and Tribunals Service (HMCTS)'s much criticised and delayed £1.3bn programme of modernisation and digital reform commenced in 2016 (HMCTS 2023c; Public Accounts Committee 2023).[1] These include: the Single Justice Procedure (SJP) for the prosecution of minor offences, video-enabled justice (VEJ), aka virtual, or remote, courts in which some or all participants engage in hearings remotely, as well as digitalisation of data processes. We discuss the ways in which the COVID-19 pandemic has accelerated the use of remote hearings in criminal justice, and the continuation of these methods.

We consider the implications of these changes for traditional approaches to criminal justice system accountability, and open justice, in particular. To what extent do digital court processes enable participants and the public to engage in the justice system and hold it to account? How, for example, is information about an entirely administrative or virtual process communicated to the public? This chapter also considers the digital context outside the court room: how is justice system data being collected, processed and disseminated online, by different public and private sector actors?

In this chapter, we also look at equality of access to digital justice systems, in terms of funding, technological and legal literacy, as well as access to tools. In this context, we discuss power relationships and how technology is changing the dynamic and interactions of the digital and physical court room, making participation and engagement more difficult and undermining system accountability.

Single Justice Procedure

We begin our review of major reforms to summary criminal justice and open justice with the Single Justice Procedure (SJP). As a result of Part 3, Criminal Justice and Courts Act 2015, adults charged with summary only non-imprisonable offences may have their case dealt with in writing without ever attending court. The SJP allows people to enter pleas in writing or online. If the person pleads guilty using the SJP, the case is considered *in camera* by a single magistrate and legal adviser, but without either prosecuting or defending lawyers attending court. Defendants can request that the case be dealt with in open court, but research has found that two thirds of people who are sent an SJP notice by a prosecuting authority do not respond to the notice and are convicted behind closed doors on the basis of sparse paperwork (Transform Justice 2021). In 2019, 57 per cent of lower criminal court cases were concluded via the SJP, and the bulk of those cases were resolved in a single day without any plea being entered (Ministry of Justice 2020).

In its favour, conducting cases via the SJP can streamline the court process, assisting with the exacerbated backlog of cases following the advent of the COVID-19 pandemic and reducing costs in straightforward cases. As these offences are non-imprisonable, we could argue that due process protections are of less significance. The European Court of Human Rights has accepted that due process rights can be balanced against the legitimate needs of the state, and that the level of potential punishment is an important factor in balancing where the right to a fair trial sits.[2] In principle, then, the use of the SJP does not offend human rights.

However, what of open justice, transparency, and accountability? In 2020, there were 535,000 cases dealt with via the SJP (Jones, S. 2021). If we assume (based on 2021 research by Transform Justice) that two thirds of people did not respond to the notice, this would mean that 321,000 people were prosecuted and likely convicted all behind closed doors, with no independent scrutiny or public accountability in the process. This seems to undermine the principle that defendants' 'live presence is an essential element of the adversarial method of evidence testing' (Leader 2021, p 73). Further, the Magistrates' Association is concerned that the SJP compromises openness and transparency, and its chair has said '[h]ow the Single Justice Procedure can be opened to public scrutiny must be addressed' (Magistrates' Association 2019).

HMCTS provides lists of pending SJP cases, verdicts and sentences (Jones, S. 2021) but these provide only minimal data about defendant name, postcode, offence and prosecutor, so arguably do not allow scrutiny of the process by which justice is being administered, or consideration of whether outcomes are fair in the context of the case. Accredited media representatives can access the same information about SJP cases as cases heard in open court, leading the government (Ministry of Justice 2023) to contend that transparency is enhanced for these cases (a claim we reject).[3] People who are not accredited media representatives can ask for information about SJP cases under Crim PR 5.8(7), but HMCTS will only provide the information in response to such requests following a judicial adjudication.

Conducting cases via the SJP is unlikely to increase confidence in, or public understanding of, the criminal process. We – like the Justice Committee (2022a) – have serious concerns not just about the effect of the SJP procedure on openness, transparency, and accountability in the justice system, but also that these changes reflect a wider preference for streamlining criminal justice in ways that undermine accountability and public scrutiny, with excessive reliance on accredited media reporting over other forms of answerability.

Virtual courts in Magistrates' court proceedings

Preceding SJP but also as part of a modernisation programme, a system of virtual court hearings was, in 2009, trialled in London and in North Kent. This initiative was 'designed to deliver speed and efficiency improvements to the criminal justice system' (Terry et al 2010). The virtual court pilot built on a pre-existing facility (introduced in 2000) for defendants appearing via a live link from prisons for administrative or sentencing hearings (McKay 2018; Gibbs 2020). The pilot also extended the use of technology that enabled vulnerable and intimidated witnesses to give evidence via remote live link[4] by making provision for defendants to join proceedings via a live link from the police station where they had been detained, charged, and refused police bail before their first hearing. There were, though, some significant practical differences between the pre-existing uses of live links via prisons and live links via police stations. By way of example, when appearing via live link from prisons, the lawyer would always be in the courtroom with the other professionals working in that space. In the virtual court programme, however, the defendant's lawyer (if they had one) appeared either via the live link from the police station, where they were with their client, or in the physical courtroom itself.

This, we suggest, has important implications for the process. If in court, the lawyer could negotiate with the prosecutor and speak to the court legal adviser about any issues. This holds a significant advantage for discussions about plea negotiations or releasing the defendant on bail (a key issue for many such first appearances). Virtual courts removed opportunities for these 'informal "corridor conversations" between legal professionals and court staff in-between hearings, meaning interaction between the parties could become "disjointed"' (Fielding et al 2020, p 94). However, there was a conflicting disadvantage to staying in court: it confined the lawyer-client conversation to the live link, meaning that non-verbal communication cues might be overlooked (Rowden 2013; Fielding 2020; Legg and Song 2021; Helm 2021).

Evaluation of the virtual court pilot suggested the scheme would 'cost more than it would save over a ten-year period' (Terry et al 2010, p iv). While sound and vision were deemed good quality during the pilot, problems were noted with time delays in the audio transmission, resulting in confusion for participants. There were frequent unspecified technical issues with the technology, which may have had a negative impact on court users' perception of the quality of the service being delivered (Terry et al 2010, p 17). As well as highlighting the implications for the lawyer's effective representation of their client, the pilot indicated the risk for accountability of the process. Disjointedness, confusion caused by technological issues, and less effective communication might render proceedings opaque to both observers and participants, undermining the educational function of proceedings while also making them less open to scrutiny.

Implications of virtual courts on participation in proceedings

As we set out in Chapter Two, the ability of parties and the public to participate in proceedings is not only an access to justice issue, but also a fundamental tenet of open justice. If people are easily able to engage with proceedings, those proceedings are more likely to provide public legal education and justice system accountability. What, then, are the implications for participation of a move to virtual courts?

Practical benefits of using virtual courts include improving access for people who live in communities far from their local court, reduced 'risk of violence or intimidation towards vulnerable parties, increased access to services (such as interpreting), reduced time spent in travel [...] avoiding prison transport, multiple searches and waiting in prison holding cells' (Rossner and Tait 2023, p 3; see also Bandes and Feigenson 2020). Despite the positive effects, there can also be significant non-economic costs in terms of the fairness of proceedings. Defence lawyers reported that it was more difficult to take instructions from clients, and to build a rapport with them, when using virtual court facilities (Rowden 2013). Physical separation increased communication difficulties between participants, and the virtual courts delivered an appearance of 'hasty justice' (Terry et al 2010, p 22).

Additionally, the virtual process was perceived to carry less authority than the traditional process, the proportion of guilty pleas received and custodial sentences imposed was higher in virtual courts than traditional courts, and the rate of defendant legal representation was lower (Terry et al 2010). Fielding et al (2020) noted an increase in the severity of offence type in video-enabled courts, which may reflect a degree of 'up-charging' in these hearings. Alternatively, it may be that appearing via video link simply results in harsher outcomes because remote participants are less able to engage in proceedings. For example, research on bail hearings and on deportation hearings in the United States found that defendants were subject to more severe outcomes when appearing via video link and suggested that these outcomes resulted from poorer levels of engagement with proceedings (Rossner and Tait 2023). Lower levels of engagement with proceedings might impact the ability of the justice system to deter future offending, while also undermining broader purposes of open justice, including public legal education.

Worryingly, evidence 'hinted that many defendants who appeared via virtual court were confused and uncertain about what exactly it was that they were taking part in', that is, they had not understood they were formally appearing in a court at all (Rowden 2013, p 103). The use of virtual, remote or VEJ hearings represents 'disruptions in the conceptualisation of legal space' (Mulcahy and Rowden 2019, p 23). Given that significant numbers of defendants experience heightened vulnerability, this additional layer of confusion further shifts power away from the accused as an active participant in the process. The potential for lack of understanding not only has implications for public legal education, but also makes it highly unlikely that a user would have recourse to accountability tools.

The previous issues are exacerbated for people who experience digital exclusion. In 2018, law reform and human rights charity JUSTICE reported that over 11 million adults lack 'basic digital skills' (p 7), noting further that the most vulnerable in society – such as detainees and people experiencing homelessness – were more likely to be digitally excluded, for whom basic internet access is insufficient to enable participation. This seems to be especially problematic in the context of magistrates' concerns that it is more difficult to identify vulnerability during remote proceedings (Magistrates' Association 2022).

Studies continue to show that 'separation from the courtroom could undermine the sense of solemnity' (Fielding et al 2020, p 103) which – by implication – might also undermine the educational function of open proceedings. One study revealed examples of remote participants 'having their hoods up, visibly smoking on camera and slumping in their chairs. An example included a male defendant appearing in an online hearing "bare chested" and visibly drinking a takeaway coffee' (Long 2021, p 92). A recent evaluation of remote courts also reported that 'interviews with professionals identified some rare examples of public users joining the hearing from locations that were not considered appropriate, such as parks, walking down a street, driving up a motorway, in a public phone box and on a plane' (Clark 2021, p 29). Participants in these studies felt that such incidents undermined the solemnity, disciplining, and deterrent effect of experiencing criminal proceedings, therefore undermining some of the functions of the criminal process discussed in Chapter Two. In simulated online Crown Court trials Mulcahy et al (2020) found that legal professionals 'were highly effective in creating a sense of gravitas and civic occasion' (2020, p 4) but that the rooms the participants were in (and hence the screen backgrounds) had a negative impact on solemnity.

Courtroom architecture usually provides cues about expected behaviours in the space (Mulcahy and Rowden 2019; Bandes and Feigenson 2020), thereby providing a degree of public understanding. While the ability of people to assess credibility via demeanour is contested, live in-person hearings have provided legitimising power to the criminal process for centuries (Bandes and Feigenson 2020). Bandes and Feigenson (2020) agree that parties are likely to behave differently online than in live synchronous hearings. We suggest that the move toward virtual courtrooms has eroded the defendant's voice, and that it undermines the sense of trust and legitimacy placed in the process, trivialising it and making the process less transparent in open justice terms. Despite these concerns and the outcome of the pilot evaluation, and with Ministers demanding ever swifter administration of summary justice, virtual courts were rolled out across the rest of Kent in 2012 (BBC News 2012). In 2015, HMCTS announced plans for further streamlining summary justice, in which virtual courts were set to play a role in increasing efficiency and reducing cost (Ward 2017). Despite this commitment to a program of digital court reform, its progress was slow prior to the advent of the COVID-19 pandemic (Gibbs 2020).

An evaluation of one VEJ programme completed prior to 2020 highlighted the issues for implementation. Although defendants were made aware that they would be appearing via video link, they were provided with insufficient guidance (Fielding et al 2020, p 63). Some defendants in Fielding et al's (2020) study described being treated less like a human being in virtual court proceedings, which is similar to the findings of an earlier study in which participants 'disliked the video link room, most often likening it to a box or cupboard' (Rowden 2013, p 106). In this way, the use of technology splits the space so that the performance of court operates in two distinct, and very different, places (Rowden 2013). Losing the formalities of the courtroom experience, and therefore the traditional concept of what it is to experience of justice, 'could exacerbate the sense of distancing experienced for both professional participants in the process and for defendants' (Fielding et al 2020, p 9). These experiences highlight a need for public legal education and suggest a risk that video-enabled proceedings can be less accessible (and therefore less scrutable) for lay participants.

Virtual courts might also have a disempowering effect for defendants, who expressed a sense of resignation about appearing via video link despite the difficulties communicating with their lawyers and the court (Fielding et al 2020). In what we hope are rare examples, the defendant experienced being cut off the call before being able to exercise a desire to speak (Fielding 2020) and defendants have been muted during proceedings (Gibbs 2017; Welsh 2022). Perhaps unsurprisingly in light of these issues, court professionals interviewed by Fielding et al (2020) felt that defendants were less engaged during video link hearings than in person. There was 'a sense of "detachment" or "exclusion" when participating in video hearings' reported by both defendants and their advocates (Fielding et al, 2020, p 70). One defendant described feeling 'a little on the outside', and another said 'it's like you're not there [...] it's like you're watching it' (Fielding et al 2020, p 70).

As Donoghue (2017) found, the quality of digital justice has been a persistent problem. While experienced defendants might be able to follow proceedings and identify other court users via the link, technological issues, such as poorly functioning microphones and connections, have hindered participation, as reported in Mullen et al's study (2020). In the words of one of their participants: 'Strange feeling, almost as if I wasn't there. Like a hearing going on about me, like a fly on the wall to it. People in court not looking at camera I was viewing, so it felt that proceedings were not directed towards me' (Mullen et al 2020, p 24).

Overall, the evidence suggests that, for a variety of reasons, court users felt disempowered and distant in virtual proceedings, weakening their ability to fully participate. This raises a question about the extent to which the courts can fulfil criminal justice aims of public censure, education and scrutability unless there are significant improvements made to the piloted VEJ technology and user support mechanisms.

COVID-19 and virtual courts

In 2020, courts across jurisdictions were required to quickly adapt to the advent of COVID-19. With differing success rates, 56 countries implemented a form of remote court by mid-July 2020 (Legg and Song 2021). Sections 53–56 Coronavirus Act 2020 temporarily amended existing legislation to increase the use of audio-visual equipment in court proceedings. Restrictions were placed on accepting guilty pleas and giving evidence aurally only (Chief Magistrate 2021), reflecting concerns with the defendant's right to confront witnesses in person (Leader 2021). Nonetheless, increased use of online justice procedures coincided with increased entry of guilty pleas, suggesting 'that defendant decisions have the potential to be influenced by the move towards online justice' (Helm 2021, n.p.).

Regrettably, concerns about the impact of virtual courts on overall efficiency and the impact on defendants and their lawyers had not lessened by spring 2020. Defence lawyers continued to report difficulties building trust and rapport with clients, and assessing their vulnerability; and defendants appearing via video link remained less likely to have legal representation than those appearing in person (Fielding et al 2020; Long 2021). Technical issues remained present: such as problems with audio quality and stability, and synchronicity between the video and audio resulting in instances of disruptive overlapping speech (Fielding et al 2020). In our 2020 dataset, eight of 43 Magistrates' court hearings were conducted using video-link facilities for defendants (and their representative if one was present). In seven of those cases, complaints about, or problems with, the connection and/or camera position were reported and caused frustration in court. Three of our four student observers in 2020 noted that video link audio was of low quality, necessitating frequent repetition or missed points. This group of researchers described video-link hearings as chaotic, with significant waits for people to join the link and poor-quality audio and video. While small scale, this research lends support to similar studies of virtual court proceedings, all of which report problems with communication that detrimentally impact user participation, and, as a result, restrict access to justice and scrutiny of proceedings.

With the emergency shift to online proceedings when the COVID-19 lockdown was imposed in March 2020, previously expressed concerns regarding the practicalities of implementation, digital exclusion, participation and open justice became especially relevant (JUSTICE 2018; Justice Committee 2020; Long 2021). A study during that period found that 44 per cent of participants felt that it was significantly more difficult for defendants to participate in proceedings conducted remotely, while 67 per cent of respondents believed

> remote hearings had a significant negative impact on the ability of defendants and their lawyers to communicate before and during hearings […] and 60 per cent of respondents expressed that the use of video link or telephone had a noticeably negative impact on the overall fairness of the hearings. (Fair Trials 2020, p 7)

Lack of access to devices (meaning that sometimes participation could only occur aurally) and a lack of knowledge about how to use software seemed to cause particular problems during this time (Clark 2021; Long 2021), symptomatic of a system reacting to an unexpected crisis.

Camera positioning continued to contribute to a sense of detachment from proceedings because court users were unable to view the whole courtroom, including the public gallery (Fielding et al 2020), from which defendants might otherwise receive a reassuring gesture from friends or family (Rowden 2013). On the other hand, Mulcahy et al (2020) found that lay participants had a better view of proceedings and felt a greater sense of engagement in simulated online jury trials. An important factor in this different finding may be the presence of *all* participants virtually, rather than only the defendant (potentially alongside their lawyer) in a hybrid format. Rossner and Tait (2023, p 18) point to the significance of this arrangement and explained that a 'distributed courtroom' (where *all* participants appear remotely) 'can communicate a sense of equality and shared experience among remote participants in a criminal hearing'. In courtrooms where only the defendant is appearing remotely, they can become isolated and experience restricted communication; the format 'can increase stress among people who are already vulnerable' (Rossner and Tate 2023, p 3). Beyond the immediate effect on a defendant's case, we suggest there is likely to be a wider impact on accountability: with restricted transparency and communication, it becomes harder for the parties and third-party observers to hold proceedings to account.

Evaluation of the rapid move to extensive virtual courts suggested that the use of video link technology might affect the ability of participants and the public to properly engage with proceedings. In Long's study – conducted shortly after the pandemic began – lawyer participants expressed the view that 'their clients were less able to engage in proceedings, explaining that even being placed in a dock at the back of the courtroom was preferable to appearing remotely because "on a screen you actually feel far" given the low quality and bad framing of the court cameras' (2021, p 94).

A rapid evaluation by HMCTS surveyed 4,808 public users who took part in remote hearings between May and October 2020; however, only ten per cent of those surveyed were a party to Magistrates' court proceedings and eight per cent of those surveyed were a party to Crown Court proceedings (Clark 2021). The 3,777 public Magistrates' court users sampled by HMCTS represents 0.04 per cent of the 1.04 million cases that Magistrates' courts disposed of in 2020 (Ministry of Justice 2021a), so the data must be read with care in relation to criminal courts. Nonetheless, the evaluation revealed a general continuation of themes highlighted in previous studies about remote hearings, such as: problems building rapport and taking instructions when legal representatives and clients were not co-located; concerns about privacy; difficulties assessing non-verbal cues and in communicating with other representatives or parties (and thereby potentially resolve issues) before hearings.

Separate research revealed '[p]oor internet connections, unreliable technology and a lack of user familiarity with the new systems meant that remote hearings did not routinely proceed smoothly in Magistrates' courts where low-grade equipment and poor Wi-Fi provision was endemic' (Godfrey et al 2022, p 1047). Specifically in criminal proceedings, judges 'were less likely to report being able to communicate effectively with public users [and] were more likely to report [that] litigants in person are less able to communicate effectively' than in other jurisdictions (Clark 2021, p 60). Magistrates who were surveyed criticised poor infrastructure for remote (audio and visual) proceedings, citing technical problems as barriers to effective communication, participation, and the quality of justice (Magistrates' Association 2022). Technical problems which undermined communication 'were pervasive', (Magistrates' Association 2022, p 17). Additionally, as reported by Clark, public users reported being unable to communicate with their legal representative because a channel of communication had not been pre-arranged or was not practically possible. One participant said: 'I could see my barrister on the screen but there was no way to talk to him, so I just watched. I was a spectator really and that just carried on while I stood watching [public user, defendant, Crown, hybrid]' (2021, p 56).

Furthermore, 'vulnerable individuals who accessed their hearings remotely were particularly less likely to have found it easy to communicate with their lawyer' (Clark 2021, p 56). Despite some reported benefits of logistical convenience and comfort for users participating in proceedings from home, technological issues remained problematic in a quarter of Magistrates' and Crown Court cases reported in the rapid evaluation, with common problems relating to audio/visual quality and loss of connection (Clark 2021). Only 30 per cent of public users who had attended remotely in Crown or Magistrates' court proceedings felt that they had been able to express their views during the hearing, and 39 per cent felt that their views were considered during the hearing (Clark 2021).

Overall, the available evidence suggests that defendants' ability to participate is hindered when appearing via virtual courts. Flower (2023) also identified (Swedish) judicial frustrations with poor quality live-link connection, highlighting that physical courtrooms provide more transparent environments than virtual courts. In light of all this evidence, the Magistrates' Association has argued that a 'continued heavy reliance on [remote hearings] is not in the interests of justice' (2022, p 21). Rowden's observation appears to hold true: 'while "access to justice" is often cited as the key reason for implementing videoconferencing technology and promoting the concept of virtual courts, real access to justice will only be achieved when remote participation does not equate to diminished participation' (2013, p 109).

Again, we suggest that inhibited communication and participation for court users captured in these reviews has a bearing for the accountability and transparency of proceedings. At the very least, it may damage participants' view of proceedings as transparent and legitimate.

Here, though, we must insert a caveat. As described previously, the position could be different were all parties to appear remotely in a distributed court and if spaces were created where co-presence is possible. It is possible, as contended by Rossner and Tait (2023) – drawing on research conducted in France and in the Netherlands – to create spaces of 'co-presence' made possible by adjusting camera angles, specialised interpersonal skills training, and arranging screen views in such a way as to avoid remote participants feeling alienated. During the COVID-19 pandemic a distributed court model was commonly used in England and Wales, with all parties appearing online in gallery format on a single screen via the Cloud Video Platform (CVP).[5] However, even in a distributed court there is a need to take steps that will 'promote inclusion and effective participation. This can be achieved with simple changes to the court ritual to signal subtle cues of inclusion, such as an expanded welcome, introductions, signposting' (Rossner and Tait 2023, p 18). Such approaches would make proceedings more accessible, and therefore more scrutable.

Despite the potential benefits of the distributed court model, as COVID-19 lockdowns eased, there seems to have been a return to the former mode of virtual court proceedings, where only the defendant (and possibly their lawyer) appears remotely in proceedings. When we resumed observation of Magistrates' courts in March 2022, defendants appeared remotely in only three of 40 observed hearings. However, in five (of 40) cases, parties other than the defendant appeared remotely (with the defendant appearing in person in court). In one case the virtual attendee was a prosecutor, in another it was a defence representative. Two probation officers appeared via video link, and one witness appeared via video link.

If this pattern proves to be more widespread, it indicates a slight shift in the way that remote technology will come to be used, with greater use of hybrid courts for parties other than defendants. This might reflect an implementation gap between what policy makers hope to achieve in contrast to what practitioners think is workable in actual proceedings (Barton and Johns 2012). Additionally, we noted that student researchers continued to record problems with connection (especially for mobile telephones) and audio quality (exacerbated by more widespread use of Plexiglass between participants in response to COVID-19) at virtual court hearings in 2022.

Observing virtual courts

We have already noted that virtual courts present problems for participation: defendants may be frustrated by technical problems and become less engaged (impacting mechanisms of accountability). There also exists potential for other lay participants, such as court observers, to become more marginalised. Enabling public observation of courtrooms 'promotes procedural fairness and just outcomes', including the right to a fair trial (Legg and Song 2021, p 154). However, technical and administrative barriers may make people less willing to attend and observe how courts function.

Preparatory or administrative hearings may be even less likely to be observed via virtual proceedings, and the behaviour of officials outside the courtroom cannot be observed in the virtual context (Bandes and Feigenson 2020, 1328). Additionally, as we explore further in Chapter Four, members of the media may find it difficult to engage with virtual court hearings for the same reasons as defendants and lawyers with poor audio quality hindering accurate notetaking. Participants in Fielding et al's (2020) study were alive to these issues: 'There was a concern that the increased use of video could remove the public's opportunity to see justice being done and that this might undermine trust and confidence in the system' (2020, p 102). Not only are virtual courts potentially more difficult to observe, but they may also lead to cost-cutting decisions to centralise more services and close more courthouses, making it less easy for people to attend local courts to watch proceedings (Fielding et al 2020).

During the pandemic, courts were guided about media access in the context of the open justice principle (Chief Magistrate 2021). HMCTS stated that it would continue to have regard to open justice by making available audio proceedings of hearings, hearing notes (on request), and online publication of court lists and information to accredited media representatives (Mulcahy et al 2020). As Mulcahy et al noted, none of those provisions anticipated 'the public being able to access hearings on-line, though current guidance specifies that requests from the media and others to observe a hearing remotely can be made to the court in advance to allow for inclusion during the hearing set-up' (2020, p 31).

The ability to access virtual courts during the pandemic was, in fact, patchy, with differing access granted to the public and accredited media representatives in different jurisdictions (Legg and Song 2021). As we will discuss in Chapter Four, despite our credentials, our own efforts to continue courtroom observation shortly after the first lockdown was implemented were unsuccessful. Transform Justice (Justice Committee 2021b) and the Justice Committee (2022a) reported that access to courts during COVID-19 lockdowns was piecemeal, with even accredited media representatives struggling to access video links. Penelope Gibbs, director of Transform Justice, sought to observe Magistrates' court hearings in May 2020, after it was confirmed to the Justice Committee that such travel was permissible despite the national lockdown. Gibbs was, however, initially refused access and was only able to achieve it by speaking with senior court staff (Justice Committee 2021b). An HMCTS evaluation report indicated that other non-participating courtroom observers such as reporters and academics had experienced similar issues:

> Professional observers [...] reported that remote hearings were poorly publicised, that there were inaccuracies with listing information, where available, and court staff were unclear on whether observers were permitted to attend. However, it was widely felt that access for professional observers had improved as time went on. This was attributed to improvements in the availability and accuracy of listing information and due to court staff having a better understanding of remote hearing processes. (Clark 2021, p 40)

The government is aware of the need to ensure open justice and transparency in criminal court proceedings. Design guidance issued by HMCTS in 2019 indicated that, in order to maintain open justice (stated as essential), the public would be able to watch virtual proceedings (but not necessarily see every participant) via terminals in court buildings with oversight from court staff to ensure propriety (Mulcahy and Rowden 2019). We are unaware of that proposal thus far being taken forward in any English or Welsh Magistrates' court. Whatever the merit of that plan, there seems to be 'low value attached to the transparency of the trial' (Mulcahy and Rowden 2019, p 261).

In the meantime, the Police, Crime, Sentencing and Courts Act 2022 makes provision to expand the use of virtual courts as well as the livestreaming of, or access to, virtual courts by interested parties. Section 200(1) allows a court to require or permit people to participate in criminal cases via live audio or video link, with additional provisions that jury members may only participate remotely from a single place where they are all together. Under s.200(4), before making directions requiring or allowing participants to engage in the proceedings virtually, the court must be satisfied that the interests of justice of the person participating remotely are met, and that the other parties have been given an opportunity to make representations about the direction. Additionally, the court must consider guidance issued by the Lord Chief Justice, and the circumstances of the case. Section 200(5) makes clear that the circumstances the case which the court must take into consideration include the ability of parties to effectively participate, as well as the arrangements that would or could be put in place for members of the public to see or hear the proceedings.

Section 198 Police, Crime, Sentencing and Courts Act 2022 amends (by inserting a new s.85A) the Courts Act 2003 to make provision for greater public access to virtual courts. Under the amended provisions, the Lord Chancellor is allowed to make regulations which specify when courts can direct that 'that images or sounds of the proceedings are to be transmitted electronically for the purpose of enabling persons not taking part in the proceedings to watch or listen to the proceedings' (s.85A (2) Courts Act 2003). Audio-visual transmission may occur via designated publicly available livestreaming premises as determined by the Lord Chancellor. This leaves open the possibility of viewing terminals being established in court buildings. Alternatively, individuals may be given access if they have identified themselves to the court. Section 85A(5) Courts Act 2003 allows the court to make additional provisions regarding either the manner of transmission or the people who are allowed to watch or listen to the transmissions (including the imposition of conditions to prevent unauthorised watching or listening). A new summary only offence of making an unauthorised recording or transmission in remote proceedings is created by a newly inserted s.85B Courts Act 2003. Failing to comply with, or breaching, a court order can also be punished as a common law contempt of court,[6] but the amended Courts Act 2003 makes clear that a person should not be punished for unauthorised transmission or recording of proceedings using both the new summary offence and contempt of court provisions.

While the Justice Committee (2022a) welcomed legislation which provides the framework for improving open justice by allowing the public and media greater access to proceedings, it was also clear that the impact of the framework will need to be evaluated soon after its implementation. We agree, especially in light of the broad discretion given to the Lord Chancellor and the court via the legislative provisions. The content of future policy and statute on this topic will be significant.

Automatic online convictions

Taking digitalisation a step further, the Judicial Review and Courts Act 2022 provides for people to be convicted and sentenced entirely online. A newly inserted s.16H Magistrates' Court Act 1980 allows the Lord Chancellor to specify, from time to time, the types of offence that may be dealt with under the automatic online conviction and penalty system. If a conviction and penalty imposed under the online system appears unjust to the court, the conviction and punishment may be set aside (s.16M Magistrates' Court Act 1980). Schedule two, Judicial Review and Courts Act 2022 allows for cases to be diverted into the SJP if the accused does not accept online automatic conviction.

The automatic online conviction procedure allows defendants to be convicted 'without any human involvement at all' (Rozenberg 2021b), representing 'a total dematerialization of the courtroom' (Leader 2021, p 81). The provisions apply only to non-imprisonable summary offences, and only to defendants aged 18 or over, if all required documents have been served. While the procedure might well increase the speed with which cases progress, there are legitimate concerns about the potential impacts of the system on users with particular vulnerabilities and who may not appreciate the consequences of an online conviction (see Simson Caird and Bartlett 2017). Helm raised concerns that '[o]nline procedures have the potential to compromise the knowledge, understanding, and appreciation of defendants, particularly where defendants have certain vulnerabilities' (2021, online). Additionally, given complexities with disclosure (Johnston 2020;

Welsh 2022), it is unclear that the conditions for suitable use of the online conviction system can be frequently met. While removing proceedings from the physical courtroom might 'potentially avoid the traumatising theater [sic] of the criminal trial', it might also exert more control; over the way defendants and others participate, and significantly undermine fair trial rights (Leader 2021, p 74), with fewer opportunities to scrutinise the system. Fair Trials expressed its concerns that the provisions prioritise:

> cost-savings and convenience far above fair trial rights. Rather than protecting the rights of defendants and enhancing their ability to participate in their legal proceedings, the Bill seeks to exclude them from the courts as much as possible, […] Further, the Bill trivialises criminal proceedings as standardised, administrative matters, incentivising people to conveniently sign away their rights […]. (2022, online).

While the government felt that procedural restrictions mitigated the previous concerns, fears remained about court users' abilities to access legal advice, digital literacy, and about the transparency of the process, including public access to information about automatic online convictions (Simson Caird and Bartlett 2017). Both the Magistrates' Association and Transform Justice expressed concern about public access in automatic online conviction cases (Simson Caird and Bartlett 2017), with Transform Justice criticising ambiguity in the government's reassurances on transparency, which promised 'a solution which will ensure that the principle of open justice is maintained as we move to digital channels' (2017, online).

It is unclear what the proposed solution will be. As with SJP, we are concerned that many thousands of defendants per year might be convicted in private, with (extremely) limited opportunities to scrutinise the administration of justice. If listings and outcomes for automatic online convictions are published (as the government suggested), some educational and/or deterrent functions of open justice may be somewhat fulfilled, but proceedings themselves – and the mechanics of the process – will remain inscrutable. This means that the operation of justice will only fully be seen to be done post-hoc if researchers are able to analyse the systems, or people subject to the procedure decide to talk about their experiences. This, we suggest, does not suffice to make the system transparent or accountable.

The publication of justice system datasets

In this chapter we have focussed on the reforms that have introduced prosecution of minor offences without a public hearing (through SJP), and partial or fully virtual hearings in recent years. Alongside these developments have been incremental developments in the processing and publication of different types of justice datasets. However, unlike the video courts, this has largely fallen to the responsibility of non-state actors: a range of different public and private sector actors control the flow of justice system data (Byrom 2019). These include: private companies holding exclusive contracts for the production of court transcripts; organisations – including the Incorporated Council of Law Reporting for England and Wales (ICLR) publishing the official 'Law Reports'; BAILII, until recently the only open access database for court judgments; Courtserve which holds a licence to publish (some) court listings data; the PA Media injunction alert system for some types of reporting restriction notification to subscribing media organisations. More recently, the Ministry of Justice (MOJ) has shared and linked civil, family and criminal justice administrative datasets,[7] including datasets from HM Prison and Probation Service (HMPPS) and HMCTS, within the Data First Programme administered by UK Research and Innovation (UKRI)/Administrative Data Research UK (ADR UK) (see Chapter Two). Additionally, the government makes some courts information available via Gov.uk; and the judiciary via Judiciary.uk, though very fractionally and varying on court type.

As one of us (Townend) has argued for many years, this piecemeal approach has been inconsistent, flawed and not subject to sufficient oversight. The system is thus left inscrutable and unable to develop public legal education. Most recently, the House of Commons Committee of Public Accounts criticised a lack of data and research hindering evaluation of the impacts of the HMCTS reform programme (Public Accounts Committee 2023, p 3). Similar concerns were highlighted in a report by the Centre for Public Data (2023) which exposed concerning data gaps ('areas where a lack of official data means that questions of significant public interest cannot be answered') in the criminal justice system. In 2019, Byrom sought to address data gaps and insufficient data governance with the recommendations of her report, which the government has largely accepted (HMCTS 2020) – though is yet to realise in practice, as indicated by more recent reports. Since Byrom's report there have been two main developments. First, the creation of a judgment repository hosted by the National Archives, to complement and enhance the offering by BAILII. An early analysis by ICLR found that in its first three full months of operation on average about 62 per cent judgments from senior courts were published on the day of judgment, with that figure increasing to just over 74 per cent when including those published late. The percentage of missing judgments may be higher, as the research revealed that not all judgments were publicly listed in advance (Magrath and Beresford 2023, p 2).

Second, the creation of a new Senior Data Governance Panel. Initially formed in 'shadow' mode, it was formally announced in January 2023, with an open application process for independent members to sit alongside senior officials of HMCTS and MOJ and senior judges. It is stated that the panel will offer 'independent expert advice and guidance' on issues referred to it by HMCTS, the MOJ and the judiciary. With a remit of 'access to and use of court and tribunals data', it will focus on four main principles: 'open justice; independence of the judiciary; rule of law; [and] maintaining public confidence in the justice system'. Furthermore, it 'will enable the Judiciary, HMCTS, and MOJ to make the best possible use of data to improve public services. It will support the development of data in the wider justice system, increasing transparency and encouraging innovation throughout government and beyond' (HMCTS 2023a).

Interestingly, data protection and privacy are not explicitly included among the principles. This is likely because a separate judicial committee has a remit for data protection (and large carve outs for judicial data processing exist within the General Data Protection Regulation 2016 (GDPR 2016) and Data Protection Act 2018). However, it is inconceivable that any advice on access to and use of data could avoid their consideration. We contend that privacy values and law are integral to any discussion on transparency; they are, in fact, part of transparency design. The omission is particularly striking because, as Chapter Five will show, privacy and data protection issues are central to individuals' concerns about justice system data publicity and dissemination.

Summary

Given the recent legislative changes, it seems likely that expanded use of technology, decisions via the SJP and remote/virtual court attendance via the HMCTS Video Hearings Service are here to stay. Indeed, video platforms are seen by policy makers as key to reducing court backlogs grossly exacerbated by the pandemic, and the technology has been 'normalised' (Godfrey et al 2022, p 1048).

There are potentially some costs savings to be gained from virtual courts in terms of time and money spent on prisoner transport (though these gains can likely only be made in the long term with significant investment in improved technology (Terry et al 2010)). For lay users in administrative hearings, there may be benefits in less formality and remote participation in comfortable spaces (assuming they have access to reliable technology). However, we continue to have serious concerns about both actual and perceived notions of participation and fairness in SJP, remote and online courts, and how these may undermine the accountability and educational aspects of open justice.

While there have been improvements in public access to remote hearings as the pandemic progressed, the emerging pattern is one of piecemeal access and inconsistent information dissemination, with experiences varying between courts, and inadequate data and research on the impact of reforms. There is an obvious resource need: for good communication between the court and public; an adjustment of proceedings to increase inclusiveness; and access to suitable technology. But there is also a need for a cultural change, where public observation is recognised to be as valuable as accredited media observation to the legitimacy of the criminal process, especially in light of the recent decline of the latter.

Notes

1 Originally intended as a four year programme, it has now been extended until 2024 (see Public Accounts Committee 2023, p 4. The programme also includes the roll-out of a new case management system Common Platform: while relevant to the proceeding of digital courts data, it has not (yet) been used to facilitate public access to data (see Ministry of Justice 2023, p 8, 17).

2 *Jalloh v Germany* [2007] 44 EHRR 32.

3 See: HMCTS (2023e).

4 For discussion about the imbalanced use of remote live links between witnesses and defendants, see Fairclough (2021)

5 CVP is among the video services used by HMCTS (see HMCTS 2022).

6 See, for example, *Director of the Serious Fraud Office v B* [2014] A.C. 1246.

7 For an overview of justice data linkage, see Ministry of Justice (2022a).

FOUR

The Role of the Public and Media in Observing Justice

Introduction

Anyone who has directly participated in a court trial – whether as a witness, defendant or jury member – should have been exposed to how it operates in practice, with the possibility of members of the public and media in attendance. However, given dwindling numbers of public and media court observers, it is not clear how far public knowledge extends: whether many or most of the UK population knows of the core principle that justice must 'be seen to be done', and whether they understand what that means in practice. Recent research by Ipsos UK (the first of its kind) indicated 'low awareness' on public access to justice information: 70 per cent answering a nationally representative poll said they knew 'not very much' or 'nothing at all' about the information contained in court records (Gisborne et al 2022, p 17).

That is unsurprising in the lay context – low awareness or ignorance could be claimed about many features of English law[1] – but the principle is also under-interrogated in more specialist contexts. For Sir Bob Neill MP, chair of the Justice Committee, despite its regular use, open justice is 'perhaps not picked apart often enough' (Gisborne et al 2022, p 6). There has been insufficient attention paid to the mechanics of open justice: the roles of different actors, the design of the channels and platforms, the financial costs (among other features). Because of the idiosyncratically decentralised and piecemeal nature of the justice system – where legal professionals and third-party services play a key role in the data ecosystem – many practices have evolved over time, in inefficient and unjust ways, without purposive design.

Important questions also remain in regards to data management: there has been astonishingly little – given the high stakes involved – public interrogation of the governance framework for justice system data, and the implication of privacy, data protection and intellectual property law on justice data sharing and public access.[2] It would be useful to repeat the Ipsos research (Gisborne et al 2022) on members of the legal profession, the judiciary and court service to discover the level of awareness even within the system: anecdotal reports of misinterpreted rules, confusion over the access process would indicate that public access rights and rules are not well or widely understood despite the centrality of open justice as a principle of the common law.[3]

This chapter delves beneath the surface level understanding of open justice, in exploring the media and public role in the delivery of open justice. Though our focus is criminal justice, many of our points have relevance for other parts of the justice system.

The role of the media

As we have already outlined, there is a long tradition for the media's ability to report on courts, subject to any reporting restrictions that may apply, and the law of contempt of court. Historically, journalists have been understood to be a proxy for public attendance – acting as the 'eyes and ears' of the public.[4] Multiple sources indicate that there is less regular court reporting than in the past, and that only a small fraction of court cases are reported by the traditional media. The evidence we have gathered over many years, from academic, media and legal sources, indicates an uncritical presentation of journalists' role in open justice and the performance of a public service. While we accept the importance of journalists' ability to attend and report court, we offer an alternative theoretical perspective, that considers open justice as inclusive of, but wider than the traditional media, and evaluate the different mechanisms available for its delivery.

During the 20th and 21st centuries, courts and legal information has been communicated to public audiences in two main ways. The first role is that of specialist court reporters. These are specially assigned news reporters who cover courts and tribunals. Depending on the size of the employer they may focus on a particular jurisdiction (crime, for example) or even one court: as of 2022, the Press Association employs a specialist reporter to cover the Central Criminal Court (Old Bailey). At smaller organisations, reporters will be spread more thinly across a variety of court and tribunal types. The second role is that of the specialist legal correspondent, mainly employed at national news organisations. This is a journalist who specialises in legal affairs and produces analysis and commentary to help public audiences make sense of key legal developments. Both professional roles are often reported as diminishing in number, though we lack reliable data on the rate of decline over the past decades and years, with no formal public records kept on public court attendance.

Typically, assertions are vague. Almost 15 years ago the legal specialist journalist Marcel Berlins wrote: 'What's happened over the past few years is that their capacity to be the eyes and ears of the public in our courts has fast diminished. There are no longer enough of them' (2009). Ten years prior to that, *The Guardian* journalist Nick Davies argued that 'the reporting of [court] proceedings has declined to the point of scandal' (1999). Naturally, comparisons may rely on professionals' recollections from their own experience: for example, in 2012 Lord Justice Leveson[5] recalled that when he started at the Bar [in 1970], 'there was a local reporter in every court: that is no longer the case' (Leveson 2012). Joshua Rozenberg, former legal correspondent to the Telegraph, commented in 2010 that 'the newspapers don't provide the service they did [in the past]' (in Aldridge 2010); and over a decade later noted that there are just two London-based international news organisations[6] that still employ full-time legal correspondents: *The Times* and *The Financial Times* (though the BBC has since appointed a Home and Legal Correspondent) (Rozenberg 2021a).[7]

Though useful, these observations reflect the decades of an individual's career, and do not offer a complete longitudinal picture. Counting journalists is methodologically problematic: there is 'no central, all-inclusive list of journalists' (Spilsbury 2018, p 10) and as we will discuss below, journalists are not required to register with a statutory body. It may appear to be 'a simple question, but there are no straightforward answers' (Nel and Milburn-Curtis 2021, p 172). One obvious source is the National Council for the Training of Journalists' (NCTJ's) 'Journalists at Work' survey (Spilsbury 2018) which uses the ONS National Labour Force to estimate numbers of journalists in the UK: 73,000 in 2017, showing an increase from 62,000 in 2011. This has not, however, been a steady rate of incline, with a fall in 2013–14 after an initial increase, followed by another rise – a figure of 84,000 in 2016 was likely to be a 'rogue' estimate, according to the report (p 15). 'Court reporter' is among the job roles in the ONS categorisation for journalist, newspaper and periodical editor[8] and among the types of respondents the NCTJ report surveyed but there is no further numerical breakdown available.

It does suggest, however, data at odds with the anecdotal perception of an occupation in decline and a contradiction between 'industry insider' assertions of job losses and national-scale surveys that show a 'ballooning' in the media sector (Nel and Milburn-Curtis 2021, pp 173–174). Spilsbury suggests that while there may have been a rise in the number of journalists since 2011, their employment has become more widely dispersed in non-traditional online environments. Relatedly, 'increases have largely been amongst those describing themselves as "self-employed", while there have been declines in front-line journalists working full-time at mainstream news organisations' (Nel and Milburn-Curtis 2021, p 174). Further, the ONS data must be treated with caution; as Thurman et al have warned that although the overall sample is large, the number of journalists sampled is low (approximately 100 per quarter) which makes the data 'rather unreliable as a single source' (2016, p 56). This could explain the 'rogue' result identified by Spilsbury (2018, p 15).

It may be that there has been a shift away from the court reporting and legal correspondent roles in traditional news organisations. In Thurman et al's survey in 2015 of 700 journalists, two per cent of respondents gave their specialist 'beat' as 'crime and law' (2016, p 26).[9] There are also new forms of court reporting and legal journalism online: via blogging and tweeting practising and academic lawyers. Green (2021) is concerned that this provides only 'uneven coverage' and cannot be a replacement for specialised full-time legal correspondents, though claims that the real 'crisis' is in the public's lack of interest in legal affairs. Rozenberg (2021a) is more optimistic, about the public's interest in and ability to navigate legal matters but considers that journalists 'have the edge over bloggers' in reporting court hearings and judgments, as they have been trained to explain 'complex legal issues in plain English'.

In 2019, the government-commissioned Cairncross Review gave new prominence to the decline in court and other types of 'democracy' reporting, though again, the evidence it drew on is patchy. It briefly cited work by Thornton (Cairncross 2019, p 21), which repeated earlier research by Moran. To add more detail: on a given day in 2012, Moran identified 82 reports in national and regional newspapers (Moran 2014); four years later in 2016, using a similar methodology, Thornton identified only 57 reports. Additionally, Thornton's students surveyed 57 newspaper editors, with 56 per cent stating that their publication did not have a dedicated court reporter (Thornton 2016, 2017). While useful, we suggest these results should be treated cautiously, as 'informative', rather than 'conclusive' (Thornton 2017, online).

Concurrent but published after the Cairncross Review, is Jones's research, which reports the qualitative results of interviews with 22 court reporters on the challenges they face (Jones, R. 2021). Most striking is subsequently published research by Chamberlain et al: they found that 240 cases heard in Bristol Magistrates' courts in one week of 2018 resulted in 'three articles, one journalist, and hundreds of potential stories left untold' (2021, p 2416). For them, it was clear 'local level justice was being conducted invisibly' (p 2416). Further research by some of the authors of the Bristol study (Smith et al 2022), provides rich insights into the experiences of court reporters during the pandemic lockdown period of 2020 though no statistical evidence on attendance and reporting. Similarly, a short analysis by Bagshaw (2019) provides supporting observations by reporters describing the decline in court reporting over the years. While these studies are valuable in building a picture of court reporting, more research is needed to substantiate the claims that are made about the patterns and decline in court reporting.

Data on the current number of court reporters and specialist legal correspondents could be obtained by surveying news organisations. Obtaining the historical data would be more difficult, and it is now unlikely a complete comparative picture can be built up. It would be more straightforward to research historical court coverage, as Moran (2014) and Thornton (2016) have done in their 'snapshot' studies. This exercise could be extended to specialist legal coverage. Given that – and for good reason[10] – courts do not routinely record the number and type of visitors observing court, it would be difficult to obtain reliable data via any official source. However, with the move to remote courts, more data about observers is being captured, and it is possible that could be used (with appropriate safeguards) to better understand the type and number of observers routinely attending court.

In a bid to offer further evidence, our own pilot research described in the Introduction, intended to broadly adopt the methodology used by Chamberlain et al. However, University timetabling constraints meant that our team could not attend the court for an entire week of hearings as they did in Bristol. Instead, our students attended on random days over more weeks. As mentioned previously, we encountered an enormous challenge when courts were initially closed to the public and then only partially opened, with the rules unclear for public attendance during the spring lockdown and no possibility of remote attendance at our local Magistrates' court (Robins 2020). For these reasons, we present our data from the project cautiously, as indicative rather than conclusive. In our dataset, of 43 cases observed over five days in March 2020, only one was attended by media reporters. This was a trial of a high-profile local businessperson, who was acquitted. In March 2022, no media presence was noted in the 40 cases observed over eight days attending court.

The general trend, even in the absence of hard data, continues to be recognised: in its report of November 2022, the Justice Committee described the decline of court reporting, especially in Magistrates' courts, as 'concerning' (2022a, p 14).

Accreditation

Although the media are understood to act as a proxy for members of the public who may not be able to attend, courts are generally open to all. There are some exceptions: in the Family courts, only accredited journalists, and more recently, legal bloggers fulfilling specified qualifying criteria, may attend. There has been at least one criminal trial that was limited to attendance by a small number of accredited journalists (Woods et al 2021). Some civil proceedings may be closed on a similar basis. But in general, and – as noted in Chapter Two – particularly in the adult criminal courts, any member of the public should be able to attend and take notes. Though it may be unwise to report proceedings without some form of journalistic or legal training to help people navigate reporting restrictions, they are also free to do so, whether via online platforms or another media.

Within the court, there is often a designated bench for the press and one for the public. This will vary depending on the court type. In Brighton Magistrates' court, some courtrooms contain only a small area of public seating with just one or two chairs marked for the press. Margate Magistrates' court has a seating area to the side of the courtroom for the press, and a public gallery at the back of the court. Members of the press have argued that designated seating is important so they can see and hear proceedings clearly. In the physical setting, there can be space constraints in which case journalists may have to pre-register places in the court, and for bigger cases, overspill rooms may be used with proceedings relayed over video-link to a larger group of press and public. In the remote context, no such constraints apply, but courts have been known to limit the number of people who can virtually attend (Townend and Magrath 2021). On one of our visits to a Crown Court case being heard in the Magistrates' court building, there was insufficient room to accommodate all the public observers who wished to attend (possibly members of the participant's families). In the single case our students observed that had media presence, some reporters needed to sit on the lawyers' benches due to lack of alternative space.

Historically, there has been no formal accreditation required for observing most courts as either a member of the public or as a journalist. The judge or magistrate may – directly or via the clerk – inquire about the background and motivation of public observers (as happened during our court visits), but this may be out of curiosity rather than any sort of vetting process. As a courtesy, we encouraged our students to explain why they were attending the court to the usher and anyone else who expressed interest. In some contexts, however, accreditation may be required. HM Courts and Tribunals Service (HMCTS) media guidance states that 'the recognised accreditation to identify a bona fide journalist is the UK Press Card issued under a scheme operated by the UK Press Card Authority' (HMCTS 2023b). The scheme permits 19 organisations[11] to issue press cards (UKPCA no date). It is therefore for each of these organisations to determine if the applicant is eligible for a card.

Reference to the scheme can be found in the rules for access to the family and youth courts, where private hearings exclude the public by default. Family court rules permit 'duly accredited representatives of news gathering and reporting organisations' to attend private hearings. According to Practice Direction 27B, the scheme operated by the UK Press Card Authority provides sufficient accreditation. Additionally, under the Family Procedure Rules 2010, a non-accredited journalist, or other member of the public, may be permitted to attend at the court's discretion.[12] In 2018, a pilot extended access on the same terms as the media to a specified type of 'legal blogger' (qualified lawyers fulfilling certain criteria) and this rule was made permanent in 2021.[13] It was reported in spring 2023 that the accredited media and legal bloggers criteria were applied in a Court of Protection (CoP) hearing although this is not formally part of the CoP rules and any member of the public should be entitled to attend (Kitzinger 2023).

Similarly, and more relevant to the criminal context, journalists enjoy rights of attendance in the Youth Courts: the Children and Young Persons Act 1933 permits 'bona fide representatives of newspapers or news agencies'. As in the Family courts, the court has the discretion to admit 'such other persons as the court may specially authorise to be present'. HMCTS guidance states that the UK Press Card is the 'accepted form of identification required' (HMCTS 2023b). We can see, then, how despite the overall principle of courts being open to all, there are exceptions and that, for practical purposes, the UK Press Card Authority scheme has become the primary means of assessing whether an individual is an accredited journalist.

This approach to accreditation is problematic for several reasons. Journalism is not a profession for which practitioners must register with a statutory regulator. Moreover, it is not a 'fixed profession' although some 'patrol the boundaries of the profession more strictly' (Nel and Milburn-Curtis 2021, p 174). The requirements of the gatekeeper organisations may prohibit non-affiliated, low-earning or volunteer journalists who publish court reports in the public interest. Further, and more profoundly, the implementation of a formal accreditation scheme can be seen as a risk to press freedom. This can be seen as an example of the 'privilege paradox' whereby 'journalism and the media need special protection in order to fulfil their democratic function, but that awarding of this privilege can create vectors of control through gatekeeper control of access to the profession' (Tambini 2021, p 1).

For this reason, there may be objections to being asked to verify one's identity in a court which is open to all members of the public (see Townend and Magrath 2021). It is arguable, however, that the media has been complicit in developing a system that privileges those with accredited status. Representatives of the media have been invited to participate in a consultation group which has helped advise on practical issues concerning media access. One outcome has been the development of protocol which privileges the media over the general public, even though many of the procedural rules in fact apply more generally.[14] In this vein, the latest version of the guidance specifies that:

> Members of the public (including non-journalists identifying themselves as bloggers) should not be given access to press seats and should be asked to sit in the public gallery. Unlike professional journalists, members of the public may be unaware of the legal issues relating to court reporting, in particular those that relate to contempt of court if they use social media or any other ways to communicate to more than one person information heard in open court. (HMCTS 2023b, p 5)

This is also reflected in the Crim PD 2023 which, supplementing the Crim PR, prioritise information access for 'accredited' journalists over the general public in several instances including:

> Under Crim PR Part 5, the same procedure applies to applications for access to information by reporters as to other members of the public. However, if the application is made by legal representatives instructed by the media, or by an accredited member of the media […] then there is a greater presumption in favour of providing the requested material. This approach respects the role of the press as a 'public watchdog' in a democratic society. (Crim PD 2.6.7)

This approach, also evident in earlier versions of the Crim PD but now presented in a new dedicated section on open justice, may be in response to judicial fears about wide public access to court material. It means that individuals employed by media organisations, who are more likely (though not guaranteed) to have received appropriate training, are able to assert their rights of access more effectively. Responses by the Lord Chief Justice to the select committee on justice in 2021 indicates that the press is seen as the conduit of open justice. However, it leaves ambiguities about how those not holding press cards are treated when they try and assert their rights provided under the principle of open justice and the court procedural rules. To illustrate with our own experience: during the early pandemic period in March 2020, the Magistrates' court temporarily restricted public access, and held some hearings remotely. We requested information about court proceedings electronically. Even though one member of our research team held a press card, we were denied this option, as it was considered that only journalists using the information for journalistic purposes (which they considered distinct from the purpose of our research project) should be able to access the full court lists according to the HMCTS protocol. The route for appeal is not clear and the

LCJ admitted there is no formal complaints process (Justice Committee 2021a).

Similarly, the former journalist and magistrate Penelope Gibbs, who now runs the charity Transform Justice, has been unable to access remote hearings in the criminal courts. In some courts, public observers who are not necessarily journalists – accredited or otherwise – have been asked to provide details of their professional background and their reasons for attending before being provided with access to remote proceedings (see, for example, Kitzinger 2022).[15] The new rules on access to remote hearings indicate an unclear approach: though the Practice Guidance (Courts and Tribunals Judiciary 2022) references 'members of the public' as well as 'reporters, legal commentators and academics', it is at the judge's discretion to decide if hearing joining details will be provided to members of the public or not, and it is not always practically easy to obtain these details even when observation is permitted.

Minutes of the HMCTS media engagement group evidence the ambiguity here (HMCTS 2019; Cloake 2022). The group discussed that there needed to be a 'clearer means to identify who is a bona fide journalist and who isn't'. This was 'particularly important as HMCTS reforms provide access to online material to the media on a privileged basis', as well as for allocation of press seats, distribution of court lists and access to documents, and managing media access to high profile case hearings. The meeting discussed moving to a system that would require any members of the media to present a UK press card. At the time of the meeting, the guidance said an alternative means was a letter from their editor, but this was viewed as an inadequate means of accreditation. In the discussion, the 'privilege paradox' is acknowledged, if not explicitly labelled as such:

> moving exclusively to insisting that any members of the media should be able to present a UK press card has the potential to restrict access to a wide range of people

> including student journalists, legal bloggers, freelancers and foreign journalists.
>
> In raising this issue, [blank] said that HMCTS was acutely conscious of the need to avoid any impression of state licensing of journalists but for those without a press card, the only people within HMCTS who could make effective judgements about the legitimacy of individuals were HQ communications staff.
>
> The group also discussed whether, alongside the press card, there should be an alternative system of accreditation created which would potentially include criteria on issues like media law training.
>
> Media representative [sic] acknowledged that the onus was on the industry to consider this and come up with a solution. (HMCTS 2019)

As noted above, the current media guidance only recognises accreditation via the press card system. This would, as acknowledged, be problematic for foreign journalists who do not work for UK-based organisations, and people who attend and blog about court (such as those working for NGOs) but are not necessarily journalists. Regarding the first category, this is not frequently reported as an issue, but there are examples where foreign media have been treated differently from domestic. For example, in 2014, the US based Wall Street Journal successfully challenged conditions imposed by the CPS for foreign media reporting an English criminal case (O'Carroll 2014).

A second example highlights the difficulty that observers from non-traditional media organisations face. In 2020, Amnesty International were denied access for their 'trial monitor' to observe Julian Assange's extradition proceedings at the Old Bailey. The judge refused to allocate a seat, and the organisation was told it would have to queue for one of the four seats available in a public gallery. An application to view a live stream in an overflow room where other media were present was denied, as was remote access. In Amnesty International's view the judge's failure to give 'special provisions' to a fair trial monitor was 'very disturbing':

> Through its refusal, the court has failed to recognize a key component of open justice: namely how international trial observers monitor a hearing for its compliance with domestic and international law. They are there to evaluate the fairness of a trial by providing an impartial record of what went on in the courtroom and to advance fair trial standards by putting all parties on notice that they are under scrutiny. (Amnesty International 2020)

The charitable organisation Spotlight on Corruption – among others – has also documented difficulties with accessing courts information and hearings. The basic court lists do not provide its researchers with sufficient information to explain what a case may be about, and they rely on journalists to alert them – sometimes based on tip offs from those involved. Though the court guidance permits non-journalists to attend remote hearings, it has proved difficult to secure the necessary information in time to watch a hearing: the system is unstandardised and unreliable. The organisation has struggled gain timely access to judgments and to documents (for example skeleton arguments and trial bundles), even where in the case of the latter, the judge has given express permission for disclosure to members of the public and the media.[16]

These examples show that, despite a broad conception of open justice (Rowbottom 2018, pp 132–138) its application is narrow and prioritises the needs of the institutional media. This limited access means that coverage is restricted to material that conforms to a 'newsworthy' or 'news interest' criteria, and does not necessarily include material about the functioning of the justice system or the fairness of the trial. It also frustrates attempts by members of the public to access the material to which they are entitled to in law: for example, categories of information specified in the Criminal and Civil Procedure Rules respectively; as well as their right to observe a hearing in accordance with the common law principle of open justice. The HMCTS guidance and protocol developed – in consultation with representatives of the media industry and industry groups and with the approval of the Lord Chancellor – has been an understandable effort to operationalise the media's rights of access through – for example – the provision of electronic lists subject to special conditions. There are calls by the industry and academics to extend this to wider database access (Townend 2019; Smith et al 2022; Justice Committee 2022a). However, in developing special systems to meet the needs of journalists, it has become increasingly normal to exclude those from non-media backgrounds, and the operationalisation of rights of access for non-journalists (or journalists working in non-traditional media organisations) has been overlooked.

In current HMCTS and Judicial College media guidance, the role of NGOs and academics is not explicitly mentioned. There is one curious category, however, that has received some acknowledgement: 'legal blogger' and 'legal commentator'. 'Legal bloggers' were noted in HMCTS media engagement group minutes (2019) and were first recognised in practice guidance relating to live-tweeting from court. In 2011, the Lord Chief Justice introduced Practice Guidance, which provides that in open court proceedings: 'a representative of the media or a legal commentator who wishes to use live, text-based communications from court may do so without making an application to the court'. Members of the public must formally or informally apply to the court for permission, and the judge will assess 'whether the application will interfere with the proper administration of justice' (Courts and Tribunals Judiciary 2011). The terminology was ambiguous, as noted by journalist Joshua Rozenberg:

> 'Legal commentator' happens to be the term I use to describe myself. As a freelance journalist, I am arguably

> not a 'representative of the media' in the same way as a staff reporter or someone on a full-time retainer from a news organisation. All staff reporters are journalists, but you don't have to work for a news organisation to be a reporter. Journalism is not a profession. You must not describe yourself a solicitor or barrister unless you have been awarded that title by a professional body. But anyone can call themselves a journalist – or a legal commentator. (Rozenberg 2011)

Beyond definitional difficulties, this returns us to Tambini's 'privilege paradox' (2021): how should special treatment be afforded, without introducing new forms of state regulation and control? For Rozenberg, making journalism a 'regulated profession' would be a step too far and a possible breach of Article 10 ECHR.

Despite the ambiguity, we are not aware of reported cases or formal challenges concerning an individual asserting 'legal commentator' status for the purposes of an automatic right to 'live-tweet' (and in the context of criminal cases, it may be a moot point as the Crim PD 2023 on live text-based reporting omit mention of this observer category).[17] However, as we have seen, on occasion, non-journalists are struggling to access remote hearings, listing information and documents. With HMCTS protocol and guidance primarily concerned with 'bona fide' journalists holding UK press cards, there is a lack of guidance on the position for: individuals working for not-for-profit organisations, legal bloggers and commentators, students (particularly of journalism and law) and members of the public wishing to observe a case for personal interest or another connection. Within these descriptions, individuals may or may not identify themselves as a journalist.

If an individual wishes to challenge their access and ability to report hearings, the complaint method is not straightforward. There is no central officer or office monitoring access issues for court observers (Bosland and Townend 2018; Justice

Committee 2022a). A member of the public wishing to complain about an issue at the court could try complaining to HMCTS, which has a 'Customer Investigation Team'. However, in evidence to the Justice Committee, the Lord Chief Justice said that there was not a 'formal complaints mechanism' for complaints about lack of access: 'If somebody is worried about what has happened, they usually find a way of letting those in authority know, including occasionally writing to me' (Justice Committee 2021a). Beyond these methods, an individual could raise a written query with the court or make an oral representation in court. If this fails, a court's decision could be challenged via a formal application made to a higher court. For judicial review of a Magistrates' or coroners' court decision, the observer can apply to the King's Bench Division. For a challenge of a Crown Court decision, the media has a route of appeal via the Court of Appeal.[18] The risk of these latter routes is the time delay and likely costs: of court fees, any legal representation, and potentially the costs of any party that opposes the application.

Contempt of court and reporting restrictions

Just as rules for public access are generally applicable – rather than limited to accredited members of the media – the law of contempt applies to the public at large, as well as journalists. Prior to widespread use of social and online media, the relevance to ordinary members of the public was minimal and older media law texts concentrate on publication risks as they relate to the institutional media. However, now that any court observer or individual with an interest in court proceedings can easily publish material to a mass audience, with no pre-publication checks, the risk of a contemptuous publication is considerably higher. The potential damage was evident in the contempt proceedings brought against Stephen Yaxley-Lennon, the far-right activist known as Tommy Robinson. A second trial in 2019, following an appeal of his first conviction,[19] led to a prison sentence for contempt of court, having filmed defendants arriving at Leeds Crown Court, and live-streaming material that was in breach of reporting restrictions in 2018.

At the time of his sentencing, the then Attorney General warned of the risks and urged the public to 'think carefully' about their social media posts (Attorney General's Office 2019). Though a previous Attorney General decided not to proceed with any programme of law reform following a consultation on the risks of publication by social media, the Law Commission (not for the first time) is undertaking research into Contempt and the contemporary challenges (Law Commission 2022). One practical challenge is to find a means of educating any potential observer of a restriction in place, without undermining the purpose of the restriction.

As we have noted, with the main exception of the family and youth courts, court and tribunal proceedings are generally open to any public observer, assuming there is physical space within the court room. In recent years, however, there have been examples of the criminal courts closing access to the public. Because no formal or collated records on public observation or reporting restrictions exist, we cannot accurately say how rare this is. It is, however, a controversial act to hold a criminal trial behind closed doors, so where examples are known, they have received media attention.

In the case of Wang Yam a large proportion of proceedings were held *in camera*, and the defendant (who was convicted) was refused permission to refer to *in camera* material relating to his defence in his application to the European Court of Human Rights (which was ultimately unsuccessful).[20] The trial of Erol Incedal on terrorism-related charges provides another example. Here, the trial judge initially imposed 'effectively total secrecy'.[21] Though this was overturned on appeal, reporting and access restrictions continued: the court decided that while a small portion could be heard in public, the majority of the trial would be closed to the general public. However, in an unusual set up, ten 'accredited' journalists were to be permitted to attend the bulk of the trial and to take notes which had to be stored within the court room. Following the case, the media unsuccessfully applied for permission to report further detail from the closed part of the trial.

This departure from open justice was based on the issuing of 'ministerial certificates' from the Secretaries of State. Although not disclosed, the certificates are reportedly similar to those used in Public Interest Immunity (PII) (see Chapter Two, and Scott 2016). However, from the way the Court of Appeal refers to the certificates underlying the *in camera* order, the mechanism is not the same as PII. Under PII, if a fair trial requires disclosure of evidence the prosecution must choose between disclosure or withdrawing charges. This new process means that the prosecution is not obliged to choose between keeping material secret or bringing a prosecution; it is able to do both (Scott 2016; Woods et al 2021).

There is no monitoring of when or how this new process has been used, nor is there any indication that media or civil society organisations will be proactively notified if such arrangements are sought in future (see Woods et al 2021). A challenge could only be brought if a journalist happened to be aware of the application for reporting restrictions (as they were in the case of *Incedal*, after a journalist reportedly spotted a noticeboard listing). Through *Incedal*, we see how a system for secrecy which prioritises 'accredited' individuals for access has developed without the need for statutory rules. This is an example of the way there has been 'an increase in oversight and transparency measures that rely on "trusted intermediaries" […] establishing a model that is repeatedly redeployed and normalised' (Woods et al, p 554).

In this section we have highlighted how the press card gatekeeper approach used in the youth and family courts is reportedly now being informally and inconsistently used in other contexts as well. This is through the development of media guidance at HMCTS, changes to the Crim PD, and day-to-day courts practice, but without wide public consultation or parliamentary consideration. In reviewing the current approach, we can see the difficulty for HMCTS, the MOJ and the judiciary. Wholesale availability of remote proceedings and electronic documents would essentially constitute a 'broadcast' which is problematic when reporting restrictions apply. In response, there has been adoption of the 'trusted intermediary' approach, which uses the UK Press Card scheme as a gatekeeper mechanism. Although, on the face of it, this may be a sensible approach – given the importance of the media and risks associated with court reporting – it needs further scrutiny. First, in terms of the functioning of the press card system, and second, with view to the risks to press and public freedom of expression by introducing mechanisms of state control that provide privileged access for the media.

Court reporting work: news interest and 'newsworthiness'

In these next sections we consider the differences between the different actors and outputs of court observers. If – as discussed above – traditional reporting is in decline, what does this mean for the way in which courts are reported, and what are the implications for justice system accountability and public legal education?

In light of the minimal media presence in a given week at Bristol Magistrates' court, Chamberlain et al propose a new normative model for categorisation of courts coverage. They distinguished between 'newsworthy stories' (which may be in the public interest, as well as interesting to the public) and what they termed 'Justice Reporting'. This is a perspective that emphasises the process of justice rather than individual cases (in contrast to institutional media practice):

> These are stories that relate to the operation of justice and its ability to serve the public effectively and fairly. Such stories can be contrasted with those that relate only

> to individual cases. 'Process' stories can thus provide generalisable information about justice which is more closely related to 'public interest' reporting than event driven news. (Chamberlain et al 2021, p 2406)

This perspective adopts Branahl's concept of *Justizberichterstattung* or 'Justice Reporting' (translated by Machill et al 2007, cited in Chamberlain et al 2021, p 2406). 'Justice reporting' is the reporting of cases that 'reflect the tensions of the society around them, its poverty or racism or inequality' [...] 'present pictures of everyday anger and despair' and 'may reveal corruption and injustice in their preparation' (Davies 1998, cited in Chamberlain et al 2021, p 2406).

This model contains the type of activity that has been neglected in open justice policy development. Journalists may engage in activity that falls in the Justice Reporting category: for example, the freelance journalist Nick Wallis's sustained coverage of the Post Office Horizon trial at the High Court (via his blog and other outlets), and the Bureau of Investigative Journalism's reporting on possession hearings during the pandemic, leading to evictions (McClenaghan 2021); and separately, its study of contempt committals, and the imprisonment of individuals for breaking Anti-Social Behaviour civil injunctions (see Byrom 2022). Some of what journalists do, however, may not fulfil the definition of 'Justice Reporting' set out above (even if 'newsworthy' according to industry norms and academic schema of 'news values'). Additionally, journalists' idea of what they do and serve may be at odds with other justice values. For example, Richard Jones's study (2021) indicated that some journalists saw themselves as playing some sort of role in the punitive process; others may reject this function. In the Swedish context, Flower's (2023) study of live blogging illustrated that traditional understanding of what might be considered newsworthy may adjust, with the role of emotions becoming more significant to reporters, for example.

Chamberlain et al are not the first to make the distinction between different types of coverage generated by courts observation. While defending the media's right to report all information in open court, Conley and Lamble point to a confusion between 'public interest' with 'reader interest' and that media publications may 'pander' to curiosity rather than a 'right to know' (2006, p 253). This distinction is often noted by judges; however, in practice, it is difficult to draw a hard line between the two. Who is to define the worthy properties of 'public interest' material in comparison to material that is merely entertaining, or salacious? And even if the distinction could be made, the right to freedom of expression protects less worthy speech unless it is unlawful in some way. In this context, court material is obvious 'good copy' for newspapers (Jones, R. 2021), not only because it is reportable under the principle of open justice: if reported fairly, accurately and contemporaneously, it is protected by absolute privilege in any defamation action. Additionally, what is likely to arouse public interest will differ according to local, national, and international interests, and news values are shaped by perceived audience interests associated with risk, violence, and/or celebrity (especially where sensational imagery may be involved) (Jewkes 2015). In this way, news coverage of courts is likely to include salacious information which may have no relevance to what Chamberlain et al define as 'justice reporting'.

Notwithstanding the definitional difficulties, we suggest that we should (conceptually) detach an agenda of 'news interest'/newsworthiness/news values from one of 'justice system interest'/ 'justice-worthiness'/ justice values. By this we mean that some information is of 'justice system interest' and has 'justice-worthiness' rather than 'newsworthiness' and conforms to justice values rather than news values. These descriptions capture important characteristics of the justice system that may be distinct from the potential newsworthiness of cases; this would include, for example, information about court participants' resources and legal representation, and systemic failings (such as in relation to reform issues discussed in Chapter Three). We suggest that the terms should be used neutrally rather than as a pejorative classification: they may capture examples of the successful functioning of the justice system, or its failings.

The public interest journalism examples above straddle both categories: fulfilling the objectives of both news and 'justice reporting'. While activity and output may fall into both camps (of news and justice-worthiness), we cannot assume, nor expect, that news organisations will deliver full accountability of court processes; rather they offer – in some circumstances – a significant contribution to justice system accountability. We cannot rely solely on journalists to be – as is often claimed – the 'eyes and ears' of the public. As one of us has argued:

> journalists only cover a tiny proportion of the hearings taking place each day. Further, the decline of court reporting, especially at a local level, is well documented. At a time when many journalists have been laid off or furloughed, this decline in court coverage is likely to be exacerbated.
>
> Press reporting from the courts may enhance public scrutiny and accountability, but it is also (and often primarily) aimed at furthering circulation and profitability by finding 'good copy', that is a sensational or human-interest story deemed newsworthy, which may be at the cost of other important aspects of justice accountability. Media organisational interests and those of other observers do not always converge. (Townend and Magrath 2021, pp 113–114)

Here, we do not attempt to make an argument against news organisations' typical approach to courts coverage (salacious details and all), but simply make the point that it may not fulfil the broader objective of 'justice reporting' and therefore we must consider the role and rights of other types of observers as well.

Returning to our own court observation project, our student researchers felt that while individual cases might seem of limited significance in terms of justice system interest, clusters of cases demonstrating similar or repeat issues could indicate a bigger cause for concern. They also expressed surprise at the number of cases which were adjourned (every case requiring an interpreter across the dataset had to be adjourned), the speed, and the informality with which proceedings were conducted. Student researchers left court with a different understanding of proceedings than expected, highlighting the importance of public observation of proceedings for educational and scrutability purposes. To enable this, the rhetoric of summary justice needs to change. McBarnet observed:

> [p]ublicity is not, however, an issue that need trouble lower court justice, closeted from the public eye by its own triviality – or, more accurately, by its own ideology of triviality. Triviality is not just a description, but an interpretation, an assessment, and the work of the lower courts could be viewed quite differently. (1981, p 191)

Ultimately, our student researchers felt that there should be greater media presence in court to capture more serious cases, and to capture repercussions of cases to feed into public legal education. Several observed cases contained information that the researchers would expect to see reported in news media, but the lack of regular reporting makes certain cases seem unusual and lacking in context, skewing their impression of proceedings in the criminal justice system. In some cases, student researchers felt that there were important justice system issues, but the nature of the case itself was not particularly newsworthy. In other cases, the opposite was true; the case would be of interest to news outlets, but nothing of wider public importance appeared to arise. There was a tendency for student researchers to think that cases raised issues of justice-system interest more frequently than traditional newsworthiness. We argue that the lower courts should indeed be viewed differently, and that doing so is of crucial importance to maintaining the integrity of the criminal process through open justice and accountability. Instead of perpetuating an ideology of triviality (McBarnet, 1981) about proceedings in the Magistrates' court, policy and law makers ought to emphasise the educational and accountability function of court transparency.

The public's interest in proceedings

Beyond journalistic scrutiny, there are other ways in which contemporaneous and informational transparency can be achieved – as a complementary activity. Actors from the non-profit sector and academia also play a role here. Susskind, who has championed a move to digital processes in the English courts of the kind discussed in Chapter Three (though he is particularly concerned with the civil context), suggests that virtual settings provide an opportunity for more 'information transparency' as well as 'real-time observation' (2019). With remote transmission and digital information sharing, it is possible that a wider pool of observers can access the courts. In criminal settings, we are not yet aware of this happening (except for the broadcasting of some sentencing remarks). As noted above, non-journalists have struggled to obtain access and documents from the criminal courts. However, more successfully, a group of contributors to the Court of Protection observation project, who are not journalists, have been able to remotely watch hundreds of hearings – following reporting restrictions as appropriate, when reporting.[22] It serves as another example of 'justice system reporting' with 'justice interest'.

Observers wishing to engage in this activity may be academics, specialists from not-for-profit groups, or simply interested members of the public. Another important group, often overlooked in discussions around court observation, are family members or friends of court participants (defendants or victims, for example). If the court room has physical capacity, they have been free to attend. However, in the remote setting, it is not clear how judges are determining a legitimate means of observation.

The subtext seems to be that any observer needs some kind of legitimate reason to attend. The Lord Chief Justice has referred to cases 'where genuinely interested people will ask to join remotely — for example, the family of one of the parties in the case'. Though he believed most judges would be 'pretty sanguine' about a journalist attending remotely, he said:

> 'none of us is likely to be remotely sanguine about opening it up to everybody, because you lose control completely. You have no idea what people are doing with the material they are looking at. It can be recorded; it can be broadcast when it should not be and so on. These are questions that flow into quite profound thinking about open justice for the future.' (Justice Committee 2021a)

A judge determining the legitimacy of a court observer's motivation for attending (however noble the concern for security and privacy of proceedings) marks a departure from the way in which observation occurred in physical settings. Further, there is anecdotal evidence that the gatekeeping of virtual observation is affecting practice in the physical courts (Townend and Magrath 2021, p 115). If this is the case such an approach should be scrutinised critically, and subject to independent review. This is especially important given the discretion afforded to judges in the law and guidance on remote proceedings (Courts and Tribunals Judiciary 2022).

Summary

In our analysis, following Chamberlain et al, we have detached 'news interest'/newsworthiness from 'justice system interest'/

'justice-worthiness' material in court hearings, arguing that while they may overlap, we cannot assume, nor expect, that news organisations will deliver full accountability of court processes; rather they offer – in some circumstances – a significant contribution to justice system accountability. This is even more significant in the context of (albeit piecemeal) information about declines in news media court reporting. We have shown how the courts are failing to offer efficient and fair means of observing criminal justice, even where material and hearings should be open. This is partly a mechanical rather than legal failing: insufficient resource has been put into creating the mechanisms needed to provide the levels of access than the law provides. In our next chapter, we consider the 'human impact' of the current approach to open justice, both in terms of those wishing to receive information from the courts, and those individuals who participate in court processes.

Notes

1 Indeed, this was an impetus for the bestselling non-fiction book, *The Secret Barrister* (2018).

2 With the notable exception of work undertaken by the Legal Education Foundation in its Justice Data Lab programme of work (including Byrom 2019) and in rare commentaries: Warby (2020), for example.

3 See, for example, written evidence to the Justice Committee from Ed Owen, former director of Communications at HMCTS: '[court] staff have often, in recent years, been unprepared for dealing with the media resulting in frequent complaints to HMCTS from media organisations claiming that journalists were being prevented from gaining access to court hearings or information' (Justice Committee 2021c).

4 For an account of open justice in England and Wales, see Rowbottom (2018) pp 129–156.

5 As he was then titled.

6 This does not include specialist subscription-only publications.

7 First discussed in a blog post by David Allen Green (Green 2021).

8 Unit Group 2471 in the Office for National Statistics Standard Occupational Classification 2010 (ONS SOC 2010).

9 n=699. Of those that did report a specialism; 47 per cent reported no specialist area (Thurman et al 2015).

10 It could be seen as unduly restrictive on freedom of expression and on public rights to attend court, to gather data on visitors, though attendance of remote hearings generally requires participants to supply, as a minimum, a name and email address.

11 Including the BBC, the National Union of Journalists, the News Media Association and the Foreign Press Association.

12 Rule 27.11(2)g Family Procedure Rules 2010; re-enacting rule 10.28 of the Family Proceedings Rules 1991 – provisions introduced by the Family Proceedings (Amendment) (No.2) Rules 2009/85 – rule 10.28 is referenced in PD27B.

13 Importantly, the access rule does not give an automatic right to report – these rules are currently under review in work being conducted by a Family Court Transparency Implementation Group (Courts and Tribunals Judiciary 2021b, 2023).

14 Affirmed in *Cape Intermediate Holdings Ltd v Dring (Asbestos Victims Support Groups Forum UK)* [2019] UKSC 38.

15 Kitzinger's example is of proceedings in the CoP rather than the criminal court.

16 Personal correspondence with Spotlight on Corruption, August 2022.

17 At para 2.4.1.

18 S.159 Criminal Justice Act 1988; Part 40 Criminal Procedure Rules; see Harrison and Hanna 2022, p 250.

19 *Yaxley-Lennon (aka Tommy Robinson), Re* [2018] EWCA Crim 1856.

20 This section is partly based on one of the author's prior publications with Woods and McNamara (Woods et al 2021). *R (on the application of Wang Yam) (Appellant) v Central Criminal Court and another (Respondents)* [2015] UKSC 76 (Wang Yam); on appeal from [2014] EWHC 3558 (Admin); *Yam v United Kingdom* (2020) ECHR 31295/11; [2020] All ER (D) 55 (Jan).

21 *Guardian News and Media Ltd & Ors v R & Incedal* [2016] EWCA Crim 11; *Guardian News & Media Ltd v Incedal & Bouhadjar* [2014] EWCA Crim 1861.

22 Cases are usually subject to strict restrictions.

FIVE

The Human Impact of Justice System Transparency

Introduction

Media reporting, the focus of Chapter 4, is a widely accepted – indeed celebrated – part of the open justice process and as such certain practices are unquestioned, not least the inclusion of personal and identifying information about those involved in court cases. As Hess and Waller explain it, '[u]nder the doctrine of open justice, being subjected to media publicity of an alleged crime is presented as a sometimes unfortunate, but unavoidable, price of the system' (2013, p 66). To make the court reporting job practicable, journalists accept that they will report embarrassing or humiliating details about people (Conley and Lamble 2006). But undoubtedly there is a cost and human impact to this type of reporting, whether or not it is justified as unavoidable collateral harm of the process, or seen as an unwarranted damaging intrusion of privacy. As Stacey identifies, 'with increasing moves towards online publicizing of court decisions, it is likely that the number of people affected by the online publication of spent criminal records will only increase' (2017, p 274). It is this territory we now explore, asking what is the human impact of justice system transparency, and are current practices fair?

Curiously, despite the extensive jurisprudence on open justice and a rich academic literature in media and crime (see, for example: Greer 2010; Schlesinger and Tumber 1994), there is limited empirical material on which to draw to explain the 'human impact' of criminal court reporting and justice data sharing practices that have developed over time. Perhaps predictably, studies on court reporting written within journalism studies have tended to concentrate on the rights and experiences of journalists (Chamberlain et al 2021; Jones, R. 2021; Smith et al 2022), with rare exceptions, such as work in Australia that has questioned the role of the 'media pillory' when reporting minor offences (Waller and Hess 2011). In legal scholarship, analyses tend to concentrate on doctrinal argument and lack socio-legal empirical evidence (Jaconelli 2002; Bohlander 2010; Craig 2019); and most have not been concerned with the practical effects or detail of contemporary justice system data management.[1]

Perhaps most worryingly, we have found very limited consideration of 'human impact' in policy developments over the past decade. There have been limited opportunities to engage in public consultation on open justice mechanisms and justice system data management, and official reports have present unevidenced and uncritical assumptions about the role and impact of open justice mechanisms.[2] It was assumed in the justice committee's report of November 2022 that a decline in court reporting had a negative societal impact overall (a similar assumption was made in the Cairncross Review of 2019). This may be so, but supporting empirical evidence was not provided. The lack of data to support assumptions made about open justice may be partly explained by the methodological difficulties associated with measuring media effects on audiences and individuals (Livingstone 1996; Gauntlett, Weaver and Carter 2006), as well as the limited available data on court observation and activity (see Chapters Two and Four; Byrom 2019). Despite the gaps, it should be noted that empirical material is limited but not entirely absent if one ventures beyond the legal literature directly concerned with open justice in the English courts. Valuable insights can be found in studies in sociology, criminology, penology and victimology that consider the effect of publicity and media on offenders (Fitz-gibbon and O'Brien 2017; Lageson 2020) and their families (Hutton 2019), as part of broader discussion on stigmatisation and rehabilitation and the collateral effects of conviction and imprisonment; and victims, in considering their rights to privacy in the criminal process (Malsch and Kaptein 2004; Biber 2014; Van de Merwe 2017). Important theoretical contributions can be found in the focussed literature on 'shame punishment' that touches on the role of the media and the impact on individuals through various shaming methods (Brooks 2019) and in the context of justice studies, the role and participation of the defendant in a trial (Owusu-Bempah 2016; Leader 2021).

In this chapter we explore potential implications of informational transparency and open justice for the different individuals and groups affected by court proceedings. Though this is not a comprehensive list, we have categorised the people who may be directly and indirectly affected by the publicity of criminal court proceedings as follows:

- defendants
- family members of those involved in court proceedings
- victims and witnesses
- legal professionals
- members of the judiciary
- observers including journalists, academics, third-sector organisations, interested members of the public
- other professionals with court role (example: social worker)
- non-present members of the public (as wider recipients of information).

It is not possible to consider all categories here. We focus on defendants, drawing on the literature outlined previously, and pilot empirical research that considered the impact of court publicity on this court user category. We consider which systemic issues in the criminal process might be highlighted through greater transparency, to improve justice outcomes, especially for marginalised and vulnerable groups. In our analysis, we consider both general and individual effects, and relate this to an understanding of accountability which is both indirect/general in aiming to prevent future failings and direct/individual as ex-post facto redress (Welsh et al 2021). The effect of justice data sharing may be experienced as an indirect/general phenomenon (example: defendants as a group experience societal stigmatisation) or direct/individually (example: a defendant finds themselves unable to secure employment). Importantly, we include audiences who are not in attendance at court in our analysis. Here, we also consider the general impact (example: consumers of news are not informed about what is happening in court) as well as at an individual level (example: an interested person is unable to find out a piece of information about a particular case). We consider the impact or effect on these different groups under the following broad themes: access to justice, privacy/stigmatisation and the right to be informed. Like others in the field, we also lack reliable empirical data with which to test our ideas; one of the primary objectives of this chapter is to highlight these data gaps.

Access to justice

As outlined in Chapter Two, access to justice involves multiple principles that people may need to invoke in order to vindicate their legal rights in any particular circumstances, and it needs to be participatory (Welsh 2022). Accountability is, of itself, part of access to justice, and can be achieved in two ways; through formal methods of accountability that can challenge decision making and outcomes, and through public engagement throughout the process of administering justice. Open justice and access to justice system data facilitate both the formal methods (via appeal of a decision, for example) as well as general public engagement (by allowing observation, for example). It follows, therefore, that the design of open justice mechanisms and justice data system will impact on access to justice. To put it simply, reduced access to data could inhibit an individual's ability to pursue a formal method of accountability such as an appeal, or the general public's ability to participate via observation.

We will start with the formal methods. In order to pursue a formal method of accountability that challenges a decision or outcome, access to information is essential. This information may not always be available or is restricted from public and legal use. For example, in the case of former MI6 informant Wang Yam, discussed in the last chapter, the appellant wished to rely on *in camera* material from his English trial in his appeal in the European Court of Human Rights (ECtHR). Permission was refused, and his appeal to the ECtHR has since been dismissed, including his claim that the domestic courts and government's refusal to disclose *in camera* material was interfering with his rights under Article 34 ECHR. In response, Wang Yam's legal team maintained – contrary to the view of the domestic and European court – that the information is essential to bringing an appeal:

> It is an astonishing feature of the case that under threat of punishment, Mr Yam is prohibited from fully explaining the wrongs of this case – whether to the European court of human rights or beyond and thus openly refuting the basis of his conviction. The unparalleled blanket of secrecy surrounding this case is and remains a real impediment to justice […] Secret trials and convictions are a retrograde step for any democracy and inconsistent with the values of this nation. (Reported in Campbell and Norton-Taylor 2020)

Other formal methods of complaint and appeal may also rely on access to core materials – though not necessarily their publicity. In the national security context, relevant judgments may be 'closed' even to those working within the system.[3] But even open materials can be difficult to access. This was an issue highlighted in the Lammy Report (2017) on justice outcomes for people from Black, Asian and Minority Ethnic (BAME) backgrounds.[4] The report condemned the lack of availability of sentencing remarks which could impede comprehensibility and trust. Refusal to disclose materials can pose a particular problem in contemplated criminal appeals (McCartney and Shorter 2019) and the Centre for Criminal Appeals – since renamed APPEAL – has drawn attention to the high cost of trial transcripts that frustrate its efforts to assist potential appellants (APPEAL 2017).

Lack of information may affect the process of justice more generally, as well. Earlier in the chronology of *Wang Yam*, when the Criminal Cases Review Commission (CCRC) first (unsuccessfully) referred the case to the Court of Appeal, the appellant's solicitor emphasised the importance of publicity in the criminal process and thanking *The Guardian* journalist Duncan Campbell for his reportage: 'It was only because of the publicity generated by the reporting of Mr Yam's case that witnesses have since come forward and provided the evidential basis upon which the CCRC have made their decision to refer' (Janes Solicitors 2006).

Here we see how a failure to communicate information to the public could affect the sharing of important information to the case (whether of benefit to the defendant or the prosecuting authority), affecting both the parties' access to justice via formal systems of redressal and also the fairness of the system. This is a particular issue in the national security context, where certain information may not be publicised at all stages of reporting, owing to the secrecy and reporting restrictions present.

On the flip side, can it be argued that increased access to information may deter access to justice? This is an argument that has been mounted in the context of civil justice. Canadian scholar Eltis has argued that publicity could deter potential litigants from pursuing legitimate cases (Eltis 2011, 2016; Townend and Wiener 2021, p 87); and Adams et al (2022) have considered this effect in the context of English employment tribunals (2022). In the criminal context, it is less persuasive. The defendant is coerced to participate (even if that level of participation can vary; see Leader 2021; Owusu-Bempah 2016, 2020). In some contexts, it has been argued that increased publicity could deter a prosecutor's willingness to bring a case (in the national security context, for example) or a victim or witness's willingness to participate (Van der Merwe 2017), but the arguments are more tenuous. As we will discuss there may be other side-effects of publicity for the participants, but in general the literature reflects a widely held view that information provision helps – not hinders – individuals' access to justice (Farrow 2014; Lammy 2017; Byrom 2019).

More generally, we contend, information provision is critical to effective models of justice, accountability and public legal education. Our premise is that insufficient or poor-quality information about the justice system will frustrate accountability mechanisms that are designed to increase confidence in, or public understanding of, the criminal process. But how to evidence it? In *Yam* discussed previously we are – unusually – able to show strong evidence for a connection between information availability and the positive actions of a witness. How can we equivalently demonstrate that public understanding of the criminal process is affected on a more general, rather than case-specific level?

An intrinsic problem for the researcher is that there is low level knowledge about the justice system and a lack of direct experience of the justice system (du Preez 2020). However, once the public is given further information, studies suggest that confidence in the effectiveness and fairness of the criminal justice system improves, particularly regarding criminal sentencing and views on its leniency (Marsh et al 2019). A further difficulty is that more knowledge may in fact be negatively correlated with public confidence in some circumstances. What if the supply of information has the converse effect than in the studies above and *reduces* public confidence and approval of legal processes? If, for example, more failures of the justice system are known – such as evidence for systemic biases against people with certain protected characteristics – would the public feel more confident because these has been brought to light, or less confident because they are now aware of how the system is not working as intended?

This concern is at the heart of the discussion around the use and regulation of judicial analytical tools. In 2019, the French government passed an internationally controversial law to prevent the public from engaging in judicial analytical activity – including using information from public sources (reported decisions) to identify patterns in and make predictions for individual judicial behaviour. One official explanation is that judicial profiling 'could lead to pressures on judges or strategies of choice of jurisdiction likely to alter the functioning of justice' (McGill and Salyzyn 2021, p 251) but some have also speculated that judges were also concerned that tools would reveal their deviance from 'expected civil law norms' (Artificial Lawyer 2019), with critics suggesting that the ban 'was motivated by the desire of judges to avoid scrutiny and accountability' (McGill and Salyzyn 2021, p 251).

In their analysis, from a Canadian perspective, McGill and Salyzyn acknowledge this conundrum:

> To the extent that mainstreamed judicial analytics tools reveal significant and regular disparities in judicial practices such revelations will be in tension with concepts of judicial impartiality, equality before the law and judicial competence. All of these ideals are core concepts in our justice system. A powerful set of narratives – and, indeed, case law – is built on the idea that the justice system, when operating ideally, provides similar results in similar cases: we are all to be treated equally under the law. If judicial analytics tools provide ubiquitous information about how case outcomes are influenced by a litigant's race or gender, external issues

> like weather, or a judge's idiosyncratic interpretation of the law, the justice system will be forced to respond to a questioning public. (2021, p 268)

Stressing that the benefit of transparency cannot be assumed (with issues for quality and user literacy to address), McGill and Salyzyn suggest the legal system could respond positively to the analytical conclusions with 'new and profound avenues to improve our processes and our understanding of the judicial role with a view to better ensuring fair and equal justice to those appearing before Canadian courts' (2021, p 270). They admit, however, that public confidence could dip if the legal system fails to respond. Ultimately, they reject this possible outcome as a justification to further close information (which they say would be at odds with principles of open justice and freedom of expression). In discussing the role of judicial regulators in responding to potential complaints based on new (and reliable) analytical data, they suggest:

> [d]oing nothing is indefensible: if a judicial analytics tool provides credible information about problematic judging then a response is required to maintain public confidence in the judicial system. The fact that the information comes from a judicial analytics tool does not justify the regulator putting its head in the sand. (McGill and Salyzyn 2021, p 282)

The argument is persuasive: to prevent the publication and re-use of information because it might reveal bias and therefore detrimentally affect public confidence in the system is inconsistent with a justice system that purports to achieve fair and equal outcomes. In fact, such exposure provides a rationale for publishing data and allowing analytic activity, subject to certain controls. As McGill and Salyzyn suggest, rather than closing routes to information, the response should be to address any failings and strive to improve the quality of the process, to elevate public confidence – whether through a regulator or other means.

This perspective – that better transparency over time can lead to mechanisms to elevate public confidence in the justice system – is gaining some traction domestically, even if policy exercises have often overlooked this perspective.[5] In November 2022, for instance, the Justice Committee was persuaded of the importance of the public's ability to access information, with the press release accompanying its new report on open justice proclaiming: 'Court system failing to support public understanding of justice system' (Justice Committee 2022b).

Personal privacy

Inter-connected with issues of access to justice (as suggested previously, there are concerns that informational publicity may deter participation in certain circumstances), is the theme of personal privacy. In the context of the technological and legal developments since the mid-1990s, there has been increasing recognition and concern about the implications for individuals identified in court and legal data (Stacey 2017; Lageson 2020; Bosland and Townend 2023). These developments include stronger legal protections for personal data and privacy-related rights: the birth of a new tort of misuse of private information, distinct from the law of confidence, and built on Articles 8 and 10 of the ECHR, incorporated into UK law by the Human Rights Act 1998; and more robust and extensive data protection framework though the Data Protection Acts 1998 and 2018 – implementing and enforcing (respectively) the EU Directive of 1995 and the General Data Protection Regulation (GDPR) 2016. As we will briefly describe, there are important carve-outs for judicial and court data within these laws, but they are becoming increasingly relevant to law and policy on open justice.[6]

Name searches via internet search engines are a particular focal point and indeed, the impetus for the first so-called 'right to be forgotten' case decided by the European Court of Justice in 2014. In this well-publicised and landmark case, the Court recognised – based on the European Charter of Fundamental Rights – the data subject's legitimate right to request that personal information is 'delisted' from Google's search engine, stating:

> even initially lawful processing of accurate data may, in the course of time, become incompatible with the [EU] directive where those data are no longer necessary in the light of the purposes for which they were collected or processed. That is so in particular where they appear to be inadequate, irrelevant or no longer relevant, or excessive in relation to those purposes and in the light of the time that has elapsed.[7]

At issue here was an online notice announcing a real estate auction for the recovery of social security debts, rather than a criminal matter, but it mirrors many of the concerns described by Stacey, who during his time as Director at the charity Unlock, advocated for people with convictions affected by online publicity of their offences (2015; 2017). In essence, internet-based and digital platforms have transformed the way in which information can be retrieved. Global search engines give prominence to historical events that would, prior to the development of the internet, have gradually faded in social memory. Critically, the information is returned in response to a name search. The obvious example is a new employer searching for information about their prospective applicant or employee and discovering information about a historical conviction. The conviction may be 'spent' under the Rehabilitation of Offenders Act 1974 and therefore not necessarily disclosed during the application process, but the information may still be available online: via a news website, but also on blogs, social media platforms, or other online sources. The discovery of this information may have a real-life impact: Unlock reported that it would 'often find employers using spent convictions to withdraw job offers or sacking employees many years later' even though an employer is legally required not to take spent convictions into consideration (unless the job is exempt from rehabilitation of offenders provisions) (Stacey 2017, 2015).

The ease with which information can be retrieved via search engines and publicised via social media has undermined the 'practical obscurity' of historically reported cases (notwithstanding developing protections for erasure rights, or the so-called 'right to be forgotten'). This concept – originating in a US legal doctrine – describes how although information may be publicly available, it is rendered 'practically obscure' because of the barriers to finding and using it.[8] The changes to 'practical obscurity' for court records has been particularly noted in the US and Canadian literature – despite the absence of a direct equivalent to the EU's GDPR provision for erasure rights. Indeed, research in selected Canadian states revealed that steps had been taken to try and replicate 'practical obscurity' in the digital context (Townend and Wiener 2021). In practice, however, this was inconsistent and potentially ineffective.

Though the English courts have typically rejected privacy arguments in favour of the principle of open justice when reporting restriction orders have been sought to protect personal information during court proceedings (Bosland and Townend 2023), there are automatic protections in some contexts (in the youth courts, for example) and, we suggest, a changing attitude in and outside the UK to the traditional approach taken.

Most notably this is at the stage of pre-trial reporting, where current law and policy offers protection to those under formal investigation pre-charge (Bosland and Townend 2023). In 2022, the UK Home Secretary called for greater levels of anonymity for criminal suspects pre-charge, arguing that there were 'high-profile instances where the media circus around a suspect who has not been charged has been devastating' (Syal 2022). Individuals such as the globally famous singer Cliff Richard – who successfully sued the BBC in a high-profile privacy case in 2016[9] – continue to campaign for anonymity for those accused of sexual offences. Following cases such as *Richard*, and also *Sicri*,[10] the UK Supreme Court decision in *Bloomberg LP v ZXC*[11] in 2022 confirmed the privacy rights for those under formal criminal investigation, impacting the way in which media organisations approach naming individuals suspected of criminal activity before they are formally charged.

Post-trial, privacy-related rights may also be present and upheld. In the High Court cases of *NT1* and *NT2*,[12] NT2 (though not NT1) successfully secured his right to stop Google from processing historical conviction information, although the case does leave some ambiguity over when legitimate processing occurs; the judge ruled it was not solely determined by whether a conviction was 'spent' under the Rehabilitation of Offenders Act 1974, though this would be among the factors considered, as well as the specific impacts on the individual's private and family life (in NT2's case, the impact on his young children was taken into consideration). To date, there is no guiding English case law on media organisations' rights to continue publish historical convictions data – cases such as *NT1* and *NT2* have focussed on search engines, rather than news organisations. Media organisations do, however, receive frequent requests to remove material under erasure provisions in the GDPR and it is at their discretion to act upon them, subject to further regulatory or civil action.[13]

Stigmatisation and intrusion

In this next section, we consider some specific points related to phenomena associated with the broader themes of privacy and access to justice: the stigmatisation and intrusion caused to individuals participating in – or connected with – criminal court proceedings. As discussed previously, a range of studies have documented the type of coverage and digital material that is likely to have a stigmatising impact of media coverage on individuals (coverage that is permitted as part of the open justice process). It is a plausible hypothesis that such stigma and labelling could be a contributory factor in blocking successful rehabilitation (see Chapter Two); certainly, this is the assertion of justice groups such as Unlock based on their interactions with users (Stacey 2017) Just for Kids Law, and the Standing Committee of Youth Justice (Hart 2014).[14]

There may be stigmatising and 'shaming' impacts arising from reporting minor as well as major offences. Hess and Waller's work in the Australian state of Victoria considers the impact of non-convictions, which means that the individual receives a penalty such as a fine but does not receive a criminal record. Though a non-conviction means no permanent record (encouraging rehabilitation and reducing stigma), a media report and subsequent online visibility undermines the decision of the court. There is a profound impact for the individual: an online report 'remains in the digital archive indefinitely for any prospective employer, landlord, spouse or other interested party to access with ease, despite the court's ruling that no conviction be recorded and no further penalty be imposed' (Hess and Waller 2013, p 67).

Similar arguments are made in work by Fitz-Gibbon and O'Brien in relation to the naming of child offenders in England and Wales and the impact on the 'welfare, rehabilitation and reintegration' of the child offender (2017). Lageson's work in the US shows how the publicity associated with the criminal process can impact a person well beyond the period of the penalty, through a 'lifetime of Google searches'. It can leave 'many to feel as if they are in a virtual prison'. This, she argues, is counter to rehabilitation efforts.

> Each bulk sale of data, each background check, and each Google search brings a record back to life. Restoration means bringing a person and society back into harmony or balance. The messy state of criminal record affairs is far from harmonious or balanced, particularly in how it creates new problems for people and society. (2020, p 196)

Although there may be technological advances for background checks:

> [t]he reality for the short term is that millions of people in America will spend the rest of their lives digitally marked, their identities warehoused into vast collections of mugshots, jailhouse rosters, and court documents. There is no easy escape from digital punishment – punishment that is perpetual and not determined by judge or jury. (p 199)

It is important to note that it is not only the convicted who can be impacted in this way. There may be an enduring effect of publicity even for individuals found not guilty, or for whose case is discontinued. Although transparency of court proceedings is critical to ensuring that the process is conducted properly, there may be a cost to the acquitted individual: if the case is reported, or the personal data made available online, their name may be forever connected to the criminal case. And even if found not guilty, this may carry stigma for many years, or even the rest of a lifetime.

Meanwhile, Purshouse has examined the impact of media coverage on those suspected (not necessarily even charged) of crimes at the pre-trial stage (2016, 2021). He argues that there are several examples where publication of suspects' identifying information has been 'extremely damaging to a suspect's reputation and personal life, and to the administration of justice, for comparatively little gain', contending that the 'psychological and social impact of such dissemination can be particularly pernicious in the digital age, where searchable, permanent records of articles and social media posts linking an individual to a criminal investigation are easily created and multiplied, but difficult to expunge' (2021, p 2).[15] He therefore proposes – to remedy uncertainty and fairness of existing law – the introduction of a statutory automatic reporting restriction on the publication of identifying information about criminal suspects.

Purshouse's work refers to, and draws on, several of the doctrine-based discussions of this question. For example, Craig's analysis (2019) which rejects arguments that rationalise the use of real names in court proceedings as the inevitable if unfortunate effect of open justice. Building on Jaconelli's influential account of the 'incoherent' doctrine of open justice, Craig argues that open justice serves only the purpose of state accountability and rejects the idea that a name necessarily needs to be made public in all cases. This is so, he contends, in the case of *Khuja*,[16] where the individual was arrested but not charged or prosecuted. He had, however, been mentioned by name in a high-profile criminal case and therefore unless a reporting restriction applied (as it did before being lifted by the United Kingdom Supreme Court (UKSC)) could be publicly named in connection with the case. Craig suggests that as a 'direct result of his identification in the press in connection with this case, Mr Khuja may face extraordinary and wholly unmerited social and relational hardship for the rest of his life, for something he did not do' (2019, p 138). There is, in fact, some limited evidence to support Craig's supposition. In a later article, Craig (with Phillipson) describes receiving a '(wholly unsolicited) email from Mr Khuja shortly after that note was published, confirming the damage that the reporting had inflicted on his life' – both in terms of his professional and personal life (2021, pp 159–160).

Despite these important contributions, there is a need for more extensive qualitative and quantitative data in the context of media and socio-legal scholarship. Hart's work on child offenders and anonymity found no 'systematic research into the impact that the experience of being publicly "named and shamed" has on children's safety, future behaviour or life chances' (2014, p 5). One explanation for the scarcity of present data is that it is methodologically difficult – though not necessarily impossible – to identify a clear causal link between certain types of publicity of a case and the impact and outcomes for any given individual.[17] But the methodological difficulty does not mean it shouldn't be attempted. As Hart (2014) identifies, a lack of data means the courts and media may be unaware of their consequences of their actions and decisions (perhaps explaining the discrepancy between judicial decisions on granting anonymity in this area).[18]

In a bid to partially address the data gap, one of us (Townend) held a pilot focus group in 2018, in order to develop a methodology that might be applied at a greater scale.[19] In this session, which was recruited via the charity Unlock's mailing list, people with criminal convictions described how they had lost jobs or been socially ostracised as a result of the coverage of their cases in the media; many discussed the negative impact on their family members and friends. Interestingly, many participants did not necessarily object to the principle of open justice or public attendance at proceedings, and mainly focussed on the nature of the media coverage of their cases; and the intrusion caused by having their name, address and their photograph published. Several participants complained of the distorted and inaccurate coverage by the media in their cases and said they would not object if source information – such as sentencing remarks – had been available to the public. Though this data must be treated cautiously as the product of a pilot study, it does indicate preliminary empirical evidence for some of the trends identified by campaigners working on justice issues and the likely effects identified in the literature described previously.[20]

Another area that warrants further consideration is that of intrusion. Not only may digital dissemination impact rehabilitation efforts for a particular individual, but it may also have an impact on the individuals with whom they are associated. Hart's work describes how the impact of publicity 'applies not only to the child defendant, but to their brothers, sisters and other family members, who also lose their right to privacy' (2014). This reflects the approach that is now being developed in the law of misuse of private information. In this context, the court recognises the need for protection from further intrusion that would be caused by increased coverage (such as in the UK national media) even if the information has been published online.[21] Here we see how the level of existing publicity is relevant to the court's decision; a privacy claim is not defeated merely because the information is already publicly accessible in a particular digital or physical location. The court may consider it valid to prevent further intrusion via increased publicity of this information.

Privacy and data protection rights apply to any individual who has been impacted by criminal legal publicity. Example categories include victims, witnesses and defendants (acquitted or convicted), and family members of all these. However, exemptions may need to be overcome to achieve injunctive relief (or whatever remedy is sought), particularly in the case of the reporting of court proceedings where the principle of open justice may override an individual's Article 8 rights, as in the case of *Khuja* (formerly *PNM*).[22] Further, rehabilitation provisions only apply after a certain period of time, and are limited to shorter sentences; the application of this regime was discussed extensively in the *NT1* and *NT2* cases.[23]

To date, the limited evidence – in media reports and cases surveyed for this research – is that the media has not been unduly concerned with granting additional privacy rights beyond those required by the court. Indeed, more commonly, news organisations and journalists have challenged discretionary reporting restriction orders. This is perhaps the product of several factors. First, the journalistic culture that prioritises and rewards – both in prestige and commercial terms – the publication of interesting as well as 'public interest' copy (that is 'good copy', Jones, R. 2021, p 1320). Second, because it makes the job practically possible.

As mentioned in the previous chapter, journalists accept that they will report embarrassing or humiliating details about people. As Conley and Lamble explain,

> [i]t can be uncomfortable for court reporters to be the means of causing such distress, but newspapers accept the

> principle of the higher duty to inform the community of legal processes, even if it appears that newsworthy individuals are victimised. If an exception is made for one case thought to be newsworthy, it is unfair to others. Further, the more exceptions that are made, the more telephone calls the editor will receive with pleas for equal treatment. If an editor were to grant these requests, there would be little purpose to court coverage. (2006, p 253)

This is not, however, universal. Conley and Lamble concede that editorial decisions are based on journalistic judgement rather than blanket reporting of all cases. Additionally, discretion may be used to minimise the impact on the associates of the defendant: the Independent Press Standards Organisation (IPSO) Editors' Code, to which many national and local news organisations subscribe, directs that 'Relatives or friends of persons convicted or accused of crime should not generally be identified without their consent, unless they are genuinely relevant to the story', though accompanying guidance suggests that any mention of their name in court proceedings would make them genuinely relevant to the story.

Difference of opinions may be held as to the type of information that should be included. In 2014, *The Guardian* (then) Readers' Editor Chris Elliott discussed some of the conflicting views around the naming of a child convicted of murder, and readers' responses to *The Guardian*'s joint application to oppose extension of a reporting restriction on his name – some felt such an intervention contradicted the newspaper's liberal values and undermined his chances of rehabilitation. In explaining the decision of the editors and legal team, Elliott indicated that an ethical decision might override a legal argument:

> [w]hatever the legal arguments, the *Guardian* has to be sure that its decision to go to court to have the boy named is consistent with the values it espouses and for which it

> is often criticised, not least when it puts its faith in the capacity for rehabilitation. The next time we are faced with a choice, I hope we take a longer, harder look at the options. (Elliott 2014)

Whether or not Elliott's conclusion is supported more widely at *The Guardian*, and other news organisations, media organisations are certainly increasingly aware that privacy and data protection law is of growing relevance when making editorial decisions about coverage of criminal cases (Brookman 2021).

It has been observed that 'embarrassment associated with media coverage far outweighs the seriousness of the indiscretion or the penalty imposed by a court' (Conley and Lamble 2006, p 253). Although the media should not be playing a formal role in administering punishment (see Rowbottom 2018, p 137), 'public identification appears to be used as an additional punishment by some courts' and has been used by police and the media as a rationale for naming (Hart 2014, p 22). This perspective was supported by focus group participants in 2018: one participant described the media publicity as 'extra-judicial punishment' and 'extra-legal sentencing'. Some reflected that a non-custodial sentence could be as bad – or even worse – than a prison sentence depending on the media coverage and the impact on their lives after the conviction. Such observations – especially if further research shows these are more widely held – seems problematic, as the level of publicity is determined by decisions of individual journalists and based on the available resource of news organisations and, often, their commercial motivations.

Hess and Waller question the legitimacy of journalists deciding the scope and nature of stigmatising and shaming publicity, arguing that the media has accumulated a punitive power surpassing the power held by the judiciary. They question the uncompromising approach taken to court reporting and the media's role in 'shaming' or worsening the punishment of an individual for their (however minor) crime, or even a non-conviction. Whilst they do not go so far as to recommend wholesale anonymised reporting, they suggest that editorial policies for naming offenders and unconnected defendants should be reviewed, and there should be recognition of the media's 'disciplinary power' (adopting Foucault's conceptualisation) over individuals (Waller and Hess 2011; Hess and Waller 2013, 2016).

While such an approach is commendable, it may not be easily achieved in the UK. Given the British media's record on challenging reporting restriction orders, and public commentaries in opposition to increased privacy protections for those accused of criminal offences (*The Guardian* 2022) it seems likely that further protections against intrusion and stigmatisation would need to be won through the courts or legislative and regulatory reform.

A public 'right to know'

Having extensively discussed the concerns of those negatively impacted by publicity of court proceedings, let us turn to the positive implications and human impacts in this context. Here, the primary argument is one of the public's 'right to know' (a principle that underpins access to information laws across the world). We have already discussed the educational aspects in the context of access to justice (understanding how the justice system functions as part of an objective of accountability), an approach which Salyzyn and McGill argue is supported by legal principles of open justice and free expression (2021).

In the English legal context, as seen in Chapter Four, because it is often media organisations mounting challenges to restrictions, judges have often focussed on media arguments for access to courts materials including factors such as the newsworthiness of proceedings, as well as the news media's commercial imperative (to include details that will be interesting to their viewers and readers ensuring financial sustainability).[24] Though relevant, in the context of the way in which the media operates, these arguments are somewhat distracting from the overall question about whether public audiences should be informed of details in court cases, and whether there is a legitimate public interest in that information being disclosed that may override competing considerations (such as national security interests, and other privacy-related rights). Arguments concerning the educational interest in releasing information have not been prominent.

There are two primary legal mechanisms. First, as already outlined, the common law principle of open justice. This includes but goes beyond judicial accountability, with the judges also including other factors within this principle: the media's viability and ability to report; as well as deterrent, punitive and educational effects. Second, the public's right to receive and report information as provided in Article 10 of the ECHR. Though judges have preferred to base their reasoning in the common law principle of open justice (*Khuja* (formerly known as *PNM*),[25] *Guardian News and Media Ltd, R (on the application of) v City of Westminster Magistrates' Court*),[26] this case law has been relied upon and discussed at length in open justice judgments.

The question of the extent of a 'positive' right to information (more generally) is still unresolved in ECHR jurisprudence, though being incrementally strengthened in recent cases and through the development of right to know laws (Freedom of Information Act 2000 in the English context).[27] Whether or not the public does have a standalone 'positive' right of access in this or other contexts – irrespective of their right as 'negatively' conceived (that is a right to challenge a *restriction* or *impediment* to information access and reporting) is perhaps a moot point and beyond the scope of our work here. Our primary interest here is the impact on the public when it does or does not receive information from the court.

We have already considered the impact on individuals (such as *Wang Yam*) when lack of access to information may impede their right to access to justice. At a broader level, we can think of other detrimental effects: by impeding the public's understanding of the court system and its ability to monitor the functioning of the system, a lack of access can also lead to mistrust. This was an impetus for the formation of the Transparency Project in the Family courts context.[28]

As with many questions we have raised in this chapter, we lack fuller empirical evidence on this and the question of the effects of information access (or lack of access) is methodologically tricky to research (common to any public 'effects'-oriented work). But we know through qualitative analysis of case studies, such as that of the Transparency Project, and the recent work by Ipsos UK on public attitudes to court data sharing (Gisborne et al 2022), that there is a relationship between public behaviour and trust, and reliable information from the court (see also, Tyler and Huo 2002). There is the possibility that, as McGill and Salyzyn (2021) identify, there will be a negative reaction to the raw data of the courts' work, but this in itself is not a justifiable reason for its restriction. In fact, it may be the reason for its release and the impetus needed to remedy historic injustices within the system.

There now exists an opportunity to now broaden judicial and political conceptions of the 'right to know' beyond the narrative focussed on 'deterrence' and media interest in providing interesting (although not necessarily 'public interest') copy that helps attract commercial revenue. This means considering a version of 'justice reporting' (Chamberlain et al 2021) that considers the functioning of the system more holistically, beyond the detail of the individuals and their cases (though these details may be essential to understand the functioning of the system). This was reflected in the justice committee's report that discussed an expansive definition of open justice encompassing 'information transparency', as well as traditional methods of reporting, including: 'the transparency of the administration of the courts; the quality of the data collected and published by HMCTS; accessing court hearings and court documents; the accessibility of judgments; and how the courts communicate with the media and the public' (Justice Committee 2022a, p 6).[29]

Of course, reliable and thorough academic research is crucial in informing this broadening of discourse on open justice. In terms of the policy process, it must be a coordinated approach between government, parliament, and the judiciary – as advocated by the Justice Committee in the same report 'to ensure that a balanced approach to open justice is achieved so that public scrutiny of justice can be secured without damaging the quality of the justice administered in the courts' (2022a, p 51). Rightly, the committee recognised the critical role of parliament: stating that although the courts are responsible for determining the requirement for open justice in particular cases, responsibility for how the principle operates in practice should not be left to the courts alone and emphasised that 'significant' policy questions must be tackled through legislation (Justice Committee 2022a, p 51, p 10). This reflects the fact that historically, although the court can apply the principle in theory, there have been procedural obstacles to their application. For example, in *Cape Intermediate Holdings v Dring*,[30] the UKSC recommended that the relevant bodies consider the issue of (non-party) public access to court documents, as there were uncertainties in practical application beyond the control and remit of the court to resolve.[31] While the Crim PD 2023 make some distinction between different document types and the considerations for providing access (pp 8–9), the practical issues are far from resolved.

Summary

As part of this ongoing policy process concerning the application of the open justice principle, we argue that a more nuanced approach must be taken to minimise the harms of justice system accountability on often vulnerable individuals and groups. It must be recognised that systems of transparency have both general and individualistic effects, and that restriction of information also has 'human impact': potentially hindering access to justice rights, as well as the public's understanding of court processes. We do not offer a complete answer to the friction between transparency and privacy; and, in our view, it will never be fully resolved. There will be tensions depending on contextual factors, though we do not find that transparency and privacy are always in opposition, or a trade-off required.[32] Given the tensions that are present, we urge academics and policy/law makers to consider the potentially detrimental implications of digital publicity in their design of open justice policy and practice. Systems should be designed to maximise equal and fair outcomes, and to consider mechanisms which will increase access to justice and public legal education. System design should minimise unnecessary stigmatisation and intrusion on individuals to avoid further entrenching existing societal exclusion and inequalities.

Notes

1. A richer academic and policy literature can be found outside the UK: for example, Ardia's work on 'practical obscurity' and court records in the US (2017), and Cameron's work on victims and open justice for the Canadian Department of Justice (2020).
2. For example, in impact assessments relating to new legislation affecting the treatment of justice system data.
3. A new database was established in 2019 following the concerns in *Incedal* – however, it is not clear if this extends to criminal cases or not (McNamara 2019).
4. This was the terminology used at the time of the report. The government has since updated its policy guidance to move away from the 'black and minority ethnic (BAME)' label and to use more accurate and representative ways of describing race and ethnic background (Equality Hub 2022).
5. The same argument underpins broader 'open government' and transparency mechanisms though civil society groups hold concerns that recent governments are reneging on earlier commitments to this mission (Open Government Network (OGN) UK 2022).
6. See Adams et al (2022).
7. Case C-131/12 *Google Spain SL v. Agencia Española de Protección de Datos (AEPD)* [2014] (European Court of Justice) May 13.

8 'Practical obscurity' is recognised as a legal doctrine in the US, as well as practical phenomenon, originating in *United States Department of Justice v. Reporters Committee for Freedom of the Press* [1989]; for a critical appraisal reflecting on its impact see Kirtley (2017).

9 *Richard v The British Broadcasting Corporation (BBC) & Anor* [2018] EWHC 1837 (Ch).

10 *Sicri v Associated Newspapers Ltd (Rev 1)* [2020] EWHC 3541 (QB).

11 *Bloomberg LP v ZXC* [2022] UKSC 5.

12 *NT 1 & NT 2 v Google LLC* [2018] EWHC 799 (QB).

13 If an individual is not satisfied with a media organisation's response, they can complain to the information Commissioner's Office (ICO) or initiate a civil legal action – as in the case of NT1 and NT2. Separately, an individual can also complain to any search engine or other type of online data controller.

14 Now re-named the Alliance for Youth Justice.

15 In particular, he has examined the impact of citizen-activist groups on social media (Purshouse 2020).

16 *Khuja* (formerly *PNM*) *v Times Newspapers Ltd & Ors* [2017] UKSC 49.

17 We are wary of declaring a void of evidence as we may have overlooked studies in other disciplines such as social psychology. We would gratefully receive any such examples to feed into our future research as will be described in Chapter Six.

18 Contrast, for example, *Cornick* [2014] EWHC 3623 (QB) and Mr Justice Globe's sentencing remarks in *D & F* (Courts and Tribunals Judiciary (2016). For details of the permanent injunction in the latter case see: *D & F v Persons Unknown* [2021] EWHC 157 (QB).

19 University of Sussex pilot research, 2018. Ethical Approval no. ER/JT367/6.

20 An important methodological note is that the participants self-selected to participate following a recruitment email from the charity Unlock, which has worked and campaigned on this topic (and participants may have been aware of Unlock's work in this area). Though Unlock facilitated the workshop in a practical sense for the purposes of recruitment, the session was run by two academic researchers without any campaigning agenda or expectation of results, to allow different views to be heard. For further information, please contact Dr Judith Townend via the University of Sussex.

21 See, for example, *PJS v News Group Newspapers Ltd* (Rev 1) [2016] UKSC 26.

22 *Khuja (formerly PNM) v Times Newspapers Ltd & Ors* [2017] UKSC 49.

23 For a fuller discussion on privacy rights and the criminal justice process see Bosland and Townend (2023).

24 This argument is critiqued in Rowbottom (2018); also see a 'polemic' comment by Bohlander which strongly rejects that arguments centring on the commercial interests of the media should justify publication of names of defendants and suspects (2010).

25 *Khuja (formerly PNM) v Times Newspapers Ltd & Ors* [2017] UKSC 49.

26 *Guardian News and Media Ltd, R (on the application of) v City of Westminster Magistrates' Court* [2012] EWCA Civ 420.

27 For a detailed discussion of positive rights to free speech see Kenyon and Scott (2020).

28 See the lengthy submission made to the Family Court for its consultation on transparency, providing factual examples (Reed 2020).

29 See written evidence submitted by The Legal Education Foundation (Justice Committee 2021d) and, separately, Townend (Justice Committee 2021e).

30 *Cape Intermediate Holdings Ltd v Dring* (Asbestos Victims Support Groups Forum UK) [2019] UKSC 38.

31 The Civil Procedure Rule Committee was due to discuss Open Justice (PD 51Y) at its meeting in December 2022, for which minutes were not published at the time of writing. There was mention of the forthcoming item in the committee's minutes for its October 2022 meeting. Hat-tip to Daniel Cloake (who blogs and tweets as Daniel the Mouse in Court) for tracking the committee's work.

32 See Reed 2020.

SIX

Conclusion: Towards a New Framework for Justice System Accountability

We opened our book with contrasting perspectives on the impact of court publicity: the first, originally provided by the utilitarian philosopher Jeremy Bentham and subsequently used by judges to powerfully explain the open justice principle; the second provided by a participant in a focus group who had experienced the courts as a criminal defendant. For Bentham, publicity was the 'soul of justice'; for the former defendant, it was a 'life sentence' hindering rehabilitation. The vast disjuncture between the ideal and the reality has been apparent through our research into open justice in practice. Beyond the potentially detrimental impacts on individuals within the system (which some argue is simply the price of transparency), open justice is often not delivered as the courts intend because of insufficient resourcing, piecemeal management, and disparate methods of oversight. We do not – and cannot – attempt to offer an answer to some of the legal and policy questions arising in this short book. We hope, however, that our findings – based on both literature review and empirical socio-legal research – inspire a re-positioning of definitions around open justice and justice system accountability in legal and social policy contexts.

Key findings and argument

In Chapter Two we considered some of the original rationales for open justice in lower criminal courts, arguing that the concept historically fulfilled several functions. Those functions included, but were not limited to, assisting with evidence gathering, publicly shaming and punishing offenders with the aim of both individual and general deterrence as a form of public legal education, and wider democratic accountability in the context of a lower criminal court process grounded in the involvement of local communities. (Lower) criminal courts have, therefore, historically operated with accountability (of both the individual offender and the court process) in mind, although we contend that summary justice is becoming more closed. We argued that taking a broad view of open justice allows us to increase participatory accountability. This would enhance informational transparency and ensure justice system scrutability.

Chapter Three located our discussion about open justice in lower criminal courts' contemporary use of the Single Justice Procedure (SJP), audio-visual technology and the automatic online conviction process. We argued that recent developments accelerated by COVID-19 limited opportunities for participatory accountability and informational transparency, with insufficient attention paid to the facilitation of open justice in remote or hybrid courts. This, we suggest, reflects a general antipathy or suspicion about open justice in Magistrates' court proceedings which fails to recognise the educational outcomes and accountability that a more nuanced understanding of open justice could bring about. It is too soon to say authoritatively how recent legislative provisions for remote courts and online justice will impact on open justice and justice outcomes, but it would be unwise to ignore concerns about the marginalisation of participants and the public during such proceedings, especially in light of the substantial discretion afforded to the judiciary about access to remote proceedings in recent legislation.

In Chapter Four we considered what role the public and media plays, and should play, in criminal courts. While we acknowledge that the news media play an important role in open justice and courts accountability, we argue that reliance on news media alone provides an overly narrow focus for open justice to truly fulfil educational aims and holistic accountability. Alongside news media, we argue for greater recognition of educational and accountability aims, and access to courts for non-traditional reporting methods to avoid prioritisation of (and a tendency to rely on) the problematic category of 'accredited' media for the delivery of open justice. Open justice should be conceived more broadly than the activities and interests of the news media if we seek to educate the public about the criminal justice system, and publicly hold it to account. As we have documented throughout this book, rules exist to ensure the public can access the majority of adult criminal proceedings in court. Here, however, we see a potential 'implementation gap' (Barton and Johns 2012) in that the day-to-day practices of the courts can discourage public (and, in some instances, researcher) observations.

There seems to be a need for both a better understanding of open justice and the wider societal benefits that can flow from it, and for a cultural shift in the day-to-day practices of open justice. In our penultimate Chapter, we tackled the 'human impact' or cost of open justice practices. This could be viewed from different perspectives: on the one hand, how openness/closure impacts on access to justice, at the level of an individual criminal appellant (for example) but also for public understanding of law and justice processes (in terms of accessing judicial analytics data, for instance). On the other, how individuals (particularly criminal defendants) were profoundly impacted in their private and family lives through stigmatisation and intrusion, with implications for their rehabilitation post-sentence (even after a conviction was deemed 'spent' in law). A third perspective was that of a broader right to be informed and the impact of access/non-access on media interests, court participants and interested members of the public.

Here, we confronted the thorniest of the open justice territory, where real harms are documented both in terms of non-access to information (in the *Wang Yam* case, for example, where the appellant has been unable to rely on information critical to his appeal) and also in terms of unfettered access to information (the 'life sentence' and 'extra-judicial punishment' of online publicity recounted by the focus group participants, for example). How, then, to achieve the fairest outcomes from the system? Here we acknowledged that we could not offer a complete answer to the friction between transparency and privacy that is often – though not always – present. Instead, we must look to encourage evidence-based initiatives that increase the likelihood of equal and fair outcomes and minimise unnecessary harm that may further entrench societal discrimination (as evidenced in the Lammy Report 2017).

A new framework for justice system accountability: justice-worthiness

As will now be evident to readers, we understand traditional news media to take an important but more narrow focus on open justice, and one that tends to prioritise the public shaming element of open justice. When we were conducting our court observations, we suggested – based on previous studies of news values (see Jewkes 2015; Flower 2023) – that items of high newsworthy interest would feature: crimes of greater severity/seriousness; complex cases; those cases involving someone with a public profile as any party to proceedings, or in which the alleged offence has occurred in a place of public interest; cases which exhibit an unusual feature in terms of allegation or evidence; or a combination of any/all of these factors. As readers can see, these descriptors lean towards cases which may be considered 'sensational' because they are likely to elicit a wider public reaction to the crime or to the people involved in the alleged offence. We consider this to be a relatively narrow approach to open justice and one that is not well suited to exposing systemic issues or injustices. We also consider that this approach is not as conducive to scrutinising the work of the judiciary as it could be. We thus agree with Chamberlain et al (2021) that reporting on justice issues should include 'process' stories of public interest that relate to the operation of justice, as well as individualised cases.

In this context, traditional media reporting of lower criminal court proceedings is potentially too inconsistent and niche to fulfil the educational and scrutability purposes of open justice that we advocate. To be clear, none of this is to say that traditional media reporting does not fulfil an important role, but we would like to see a broader use of that role, and one that takes into greater account the wider purposes of open justice, alongside encouraging more and easier public access to (lower) criminal court proceedings.

Consequently, we advocate for an understanding of open justice which looks beyond the news media for informational transparency and encourages (or at least better understands and tolerates) accountability through public participation in the court process; that is participatory accountability. Refocussing the rationale for open justice has the potential to prioritise systemic scrutiny and systemic public legal education over narrowly focussed defendant punishment motivated by deterrent 'shaming'. Whether or not one agrees ideologically with such a punitive approach, its effectiveness as a means of deterrent seems to be assumed rather than empirically proven, as we discussed in Chapters Two and Five. To assist refocussing the open justice rationale, we use the term 'justice-worthiness'. As set out in Chapter Four, justice-worthiness describes important characteristics of the justice system that may be distinct from the potential newsworthiness of cases. This could include, for example, systemic information about court participants' resources and legal representation, and/or systemic failings in the justice system (such as in relation to the inefficient and alienating widespread use of video technology in summary criminal courts described in Chapter Three). We suggest that discussion about these issues should be in the wider public domain on the basis that they provide the public with an understanding about the operation of the criminal justice system and provide opportunities to change systems that may widely be considered unfair. As will be apparent, a central tenet of this approach is that it is important for *all* participants in proceedings, not least the judges, to know that there is the possibility of media and public scrutiny of what occurs in the court process. It can help to expose instances of judicial incompetence, unfair treatment of participants and inadequate resources: system failures that might otherwise go unchecked.

Systemic justice issues that could be of interest to the wider public include:

- Significant delays in court proceedings. Indeed, we have seen greater levels of reporting about such issues in the context of the court business backlog exacerbated by the COVID-19 pandemic, and barristers' industrial action in 2022 (for example Deardon 2022; Reed 2022; see also Public Accounts Committee 2023).
- Levels of legal representation and frustrations experienced around access to publicly funded representation, especially in the context of economic crisis, funding cuts, and vulnerabilities experienced by the defendant population and lawyers' industrial action.
- Inappropriate behaviour exhibited by court officials, lawyers and officials ancillary to the court process such as probation officers and the police. This could include discriminatory practices, illegal behaviours, or errors in law and procedure.

- Concerns about the way particular types of offending behaviour is processed and managed, indicating systemic misunderstanding or impropriety.

Highlighting these issues, alone or in combination, could help increase public legal education about how the criminal process is supposed to operate. If systemic issues are identified, publicity of subsequent responses by relevant bodies could help increase accountability and public confidence in the process, especially if responses are shown to be effective. Ultimately, such public knowledge and understanding should help to make the criminal process fairer overall, thereby increasing peoples' tendency to comply with the agencies of the criminal process (Tyler and Huo 2002). If measures were to be implemented that encouraged accountability through open justice, a more effective version of Mulcahy and Rowden's 'reverse panopticon' in which the many view the few (2019, p 259) might exist.

We also believe that public legal education is an important aspect of open justice, and one that forms part of the access to justice agenda, as discussed in Chapter Two. We suggest that, by better informing the public about legal processes and principles, an approach of open justice can encourage greater levels of understanding about the functions of the criminal justice system. This could encourage greater participation and create more opportunities for people to (correctly) assert their legal rights. This is especially important in the context of extensive and sustained cuts to publicly funded representation throughout the justice system (Robins and Newman 2021; Welsh 2022). We contend that both procedural and substantive access to justice could be improved by a justice-worthiness approach to open justice.

Reflections and recommendations

Overall, we suggest that definitions around open justice need to be repositioned to encourage justice system accountability, further public legal education, and create more opportunities for access to justice. For too long, the concept of open justice has lacked satisfactory coherence, leaving it vulnerable to inconsistent use in practice and too much focus on the (albeit important) role of accredited media representatives at the expense of other important aspects. We encourage an approach to open justice which takes into account the three key principles we would like to see improved in the justice system: transparency, accountability, and access to justice. Greater attention to all three principles could help the justice system to expand its legitimacy and credibility in the public domain, with likely positive consequences for compliance with the process overall (Tyler 2003). We hope that expanding the focus of open justice to overtly include justice-worthiness concerns provides at least a starting point for debate around these issues. From that debate, clearer principles and guidance about the operation of open justice could be distilled. Naturally, though, theoretical frameworks of this nature need to be translated into policy and practice to be effective. To assist with that translation, we suggest that several factors need to be considered, and will now discuss them.

First, there should be improved models and approaches to information access for members of the public. Currently, it seems that only a small proportion of people know that they are entitled to observe public proceedings and what to expect therein, and it has been shown that there is low public awareness of how justice system data is managed in practice (Gisborne et al 2022). Few people seem to know that they have a right to observe and take notes about public proceedings, and – as indicated by our own encounters, those of colleagues, and our students – find the process of attending and observing proceedings opaque, worrying, and are easily discouraged by even mild questioning about their presence at court. The Justice Committee also felt that, especially considering declines in court media reporting, HM Courts and Tribunals Service (HMCTS) should facilitate open days to encourage the public to visit their local courts (2022, p 17).

Related to this, our second suggestion is that there should be a cultural shift among court staff and professionals working within the courtrooms to recognise the importance of public observation of proceedings. In its response to the Justice Committee, the government argues better training is now in place, but observers continue to recount their difficulties via social media. Proceedings in lower criminal courts are not as trivial as they are sometimes made to appear, especially not to the victims and defendants participating in such cases. That such proceedings are properly and openly scrutinised should provide comfort to parties and to the public at large about the legitimacy of proceedings as well as increasing their accessibility (notwithstanding some may have privacy-related concerns, as discussed in Chapter Five). If the state is keen to ensure justice system processes are legitimate and transparent, it will provide the resources necessary to encourage open justice, which could even include making the courtrooms themselves a more pleasant place for the public to attend (with provision of seating, space, and training court staff to manage public engagement). That the poor quality of some Magistrates' courts damages morale among court staff has been raised as a concern (Anonymous 2020). All round investment in those court buildings which have not been sold off would be important not only for morale, but also to make the courts a more conducive place for the performance of open justice.

On the issue of investment, our third suggestion is that there needs to be greater resource provision to improve the quality of, and access to, virtual court proceedings, video-enabled justice, and remote proceedings. Given that these measures are now firmly part of the justice landscape, attention needs to be paid to the observation and participation barriers present in poorly implemented virtual proceedings, as well as the opportunities for greater engagement in the process by all interested parties. This requires investment in information technology (IT) infrastructure and a coherent policy that explicitly articulates the aims of virtual proceedings in relation to participatory accountability and open justice. The government has defended its approach and use of resources in its response to the Justice Committee in 2023 (rejecting many of the committee's proposed initiatives), but at the time of writing, court observers continue to report the access problems described throughout this book.

Fourthly, there is an urgent need for better data accountability mechanisms to further justice system accountability and fair and equal access to justice. This includes anonymised statistical data, as well as qualitative information from the courts. While the Data First initiative is a step in the right direction, as discussed in Chapter Two, its processes are cumbersome and subject to significant gatekeeping, and only relevant to certain types of justice data. This is not – we suggest – compliant with the spirit of open justice, public engagement, or participatory accountability. Instead, we suggest that more criminal justice system data should be freely available in publicly accessible areas/websites than is currently the case. While the Ministry of Justice publishes Criminal Justice Statistics Quarterly, overview tables, and bulletins, much of this information simply describes case progression activities and outcomes. It is not presented in ways that the lay public would find easy to follow, being – aside from the bulletins – contained mainly in Excel spreadsheets. For the system to be more accountable, access to information around demographics, cross-tabulated with outcomes and other indicators of potential justice system issues would be useful. This would also potentially present a less sensationalised understanding of the justice system than that sometimes presented by media outlets. It is essential, as Byrom (2019) has shown in her extensive work on digital justice, to improving both access to justice and reducing inequalities within the system.

On the media, we (fifthly) suggest that further investment is needed to reinstate or expand the role of court reporting. While we believe news media court reporting is just one important element of one justice, the apparent demise of court reporting in recent years does little to assist development of the principles we advocate for in terms of justice system scrutiny and public legal education. Grassroots groups have played an important role in documenting the activity of previously underreported courts in other jurisdictions (the Transparency Project for the Family Courts, the Court of Protection Open Justice Project for the Court of Protection). The philanthropically supported Bureau of Investigative Journalism has undertaken important projects on the county court possession hearings and on committals for breaches of civil injunctions. Although universal approaches in civil and criminal jurisdictions may not be appropriate given the role of the state in criminal proceedings (Chapter Two), similar initiatives are desperately needed in the criminal justice sector. As we finished writing, Transform Justice announced the launch of a CourtWatch project to improve open justice in Magistrates' courts, and we hope that this will encourage positive developments. Though we do not explore investment models here, options include more readily facilitating charitably funded journalism (Barnett et al 2022) or developing a version of the BBC Local Democracy Reporters' model focussing on courts, which would involve civil society or legal specialist organisations, as well as the news media.

We recognise that there remains much to refine around the concept of open justice; what issues it should encompass, and how far it should extend. Toulson L.J. observed in 2012,

> [w]hile the broad principle [of open justice] and its objective are unquestionable, its practical application may need reconsideration from time to time to take account of changes in the way that society and the courts work. Unsurprisingly there may be differences of view about such matters.[1]

We agree to a point. Our research certainly shows 'differences of views'. We would put his observation in far stronger terms: the practical application of open justice *demands* reconsideration *on an ongoing basis* to take account of changes in the way that society and the courts work. Finally, we posit that the principle and objective *should be questioned* – though we advance – we hope robustly – an argument for open justice in this book, we hope we have shown how the principle can be dissected, and the objectives tested through sociolegal research.

Whose job, then, is it to decide the shape of open justice? Through this book we have shown how different actors (state and non-state) perform contributory roles, often leading to messy results, especially in the context of ever-increasing access to different forms of social media. Oversight is, however, needed. As the Justice Committee said:

> [o]pen justice is a common law principle, and it is for the courts to determine its requirements in particular cases. However, responsibility for deciding how the principle should operate should not be left to the courts alone. Deciding the proper limits of open justice can often give rise to significant policy questions that Government and Parliament can only tackle through legislation. (2022a, p 10)

At this point, the government has rejected this call for further legislation. Though we support the committee's recommendation in principle, we would urge caution before the introduction of new legislation. If we treat the government's consultation in good faith (rather than dismissing it as an exercise in kicking issues into the long grass), there may be an opportunity to contribute evidence and ideas that lead to more nuanced and fairer policy and practice on open justice.[2] We concede, though, the current political context provides some challenges in terms of strengthening, rather than weakening, human rights.[3] Additionally – as all good academic studies conclude – further independent research is essential to this exercise. Unfortunately, at this point, we often lack the baseline justice system data with which to conduct reliable studies, and methodological issues abound in terms of establishing correlative effects between events (as discussed in Chapter Five). But we – and we encourage others to – try nonetheless, to continue what is a growing body of academic work that interrogates the principle and functioning of open justice, pushing us beyond ideological notions of criminal justice and unevidenced dogma, to fairer and better ways of doing open justice and holding the justice system to account, while minimising individual and societal harms.

We hope that by bringing justice system issues, accountability, public legal education, and access to justice into sharper focus in this book, we provide a valuable framework that can be critiqued and built upon, in the broader effort to improve legitimacy and credibility in the justice system, especially where it concerns matters of criminal justice. This objective is why, we contend, that justice must 'not only be done, but should manifestly and undoubtedly be seen to be done'.[4] That early 20th century articulation and rationalisation of open justice stands true, but inevitably its application and core purposes must be revisited to reflect contemporary societal (and justice system) values and the ways in which people share information and ideas.

Notes

1 *Guardian News and Media Ltd, R (on the application of) v City of Westminster Magistrates' Court* [2012] EWCA Civ 420, 5.

2 Indeed, one of us has previously urged the Ministry of Justice to consult on some of these issues over the years.

3 At the time of writing, the government's Bill of Rights which would seek to reform the Human Rights Act 1998 was reported to be on pause.

4 *Sussex Justices, Ex parte McCarthy* [1924] 1 KB 256 at 259.

References

Adams, Z., Adams-Prassl, A. and Adams-Prassl, J. (2022) 'Online Tribunal Judgments and the Limits of Open Justice', *Legal Studies*, 42(1), pp 42–60.

Adams-Prassl, A. and Adams-Prassl, J. (2020) 'Systemic Unfairness, Access to Justice and Futility: A Framework', *Oxford Journal of Legal Studies*, 40(3), pp 561–590.

Adisa, O. (2018) *Access to Justice: Assessing the Impact of the Magistrates' Court Closures in Suffolk*. Ipswich: Institute for Social and Economic Research.

Aldridge, A. (2010) 'The Geek Shall Inherit', *Legal Week*, 21 October.

Amnesty International. (2020) 'Why are Amnesty International Monitors not able to Observe the Assange Hearing?', *Amnesty International*, 21 September. Available at: https://www.amnesty.org/en/latest/news/2020/09/why-are-amnesty-international-monitors-not-able-to-observe-the-assange-hearing/ (Accessed: 8 February 2023).

Anonymous. (2018) *The Secret Barrister: Stories of the Law and How it's Broken*. London: Picador.

Anonymous. (2020) *The Secret Magistrate*. Oakamoor: Hawksmoor Publishing.

Appeal. (2017) *Open Justice Charter Launched*. Available at: https://appeal.org.uk/news/2017/1/13/open-justice-charter-launched, 13 January (Accessed: 8 February 2023).

Ardia, D.S. (2017) 'Privacy and Court Records: Online Access and the Loss of Practical Obscurity', *University of Illinois Law Review*, 2017(4), pp 1385–1454.

Artificial Lawyer (2019) 'France Bans Judge Analytics, 5 Years in Prison for Rule Breakers', *Artificial Lawyer*, 4 June. Available at: https://www.artificiallawyer.com/2019/06/04/france-bans-judge-analytics-5-years-in-prison-for-rule-breakers/ (Accessed: 23 August 2023).

Ashworth, A. and Horder, J. (2013) *Principles of Criminal Law*, sixth edn. Oxford: Oxford University Press.

Attorney General's Office. (2019) 'Stephen Yaxley-Lennon committed to prison for contempt of court', 19 July. Available at: https://www.gov.uk/government/news/stephen-yaxley-lennon-committed-to-prison-for-contempt-of-court (Accessed: 8 February 2023).

Bagshaw, T. (2019) 'What Happens When Our Local News Disappears? How UK Local Newspapers are Closing and Coverage of Court Proceedings is not Happening', *Index on Censorship*, 48(1), pp 29–31.

Bandes, S. and Feigenson, N. (2020) 'Virtual Trials: Necessity, Invention, and the Evolution of the Courtroom', *Buffalo Law Review*, 68(5), pp 1275–1372.

Banks, S. (2014) *Informal Justice in England and Wales, 1760–1914: The Courts of Popular Opinion*. Martlesham: Boydell & Brewer.

Barnett, S., Murdoch, T. and Townend, J. (2022) 'Where Public Interest and Public Benefit Meet: The Application of Charity Law to Journalism', *Journal of Media Law*, 14(2), pp 323–351.

Barr, A., Packard, T. and Serra, D. (2014) 'Participatory accountability and collective action: Experimental evidence from Albania', *European Economic Review*, 68, pp 250–269.

Barton, A. and Johns, N. (2012) *The Policy Making Process in the Criminal Justice System*. London: Routledge.

BBC News. (2012) *'Virtual' Courts Rolled out across Kent*, 1 August. Available at: https://www.bbc.co.uk/news/uk-england-kent-19080208 (Accessed: 13 February 2023).

Beattie, J.M. (2007) 'Sir John Fielding and Public Justice: The Bow Street Magistrates' Court, 1754–1780', *Law and History Review*, 25(1), pp 61–100.

Berlins, M. (2009) 'Loss of Court Reporters is a Blow to Open Justice', *The Guardian*, 7 December. Available at: https://www.theguardian.com/commentisfree/2009/dec/06/berlins-writ-large-court-reporters (Accessed: 26 July 2022).

Besemer, S., Farrington, D.P. and Bijleveld, C.C.J.H. (2017) 'Labeling and Intergenerational Transmission of Crime: The Interaction Between Criminal Justice Intervention and a Convicted Parent', *PLoS ONE*, 12(3), e0172419.

Biber, K. (2014) 'Inside Jill Meagher's Handbag: Looking at Open Justice', *Alternative Law Journal*, 39(2), pp 73–77.

Bingham, T. (2006) 'Sixth Sir David Williams Lecture: The Rule of Law'. Available at: https://www.cpl.law.cam.ac.uk/sir-david-williams-lectures2006-rule-law/rule-law-text-transcript (Accessed: 22 June 2023).

Bohlander, M. (2010) 'Open Justice or Open Season?: Should the Media Report the Names of Suspects and Defendants?', *The Journal of Criminal Law*, 74(4), pp 321–338.

Bosland, J. and Gill, J., (2015) 'The Principle of Open Justice and the Judicial Duty to Give Public Reasons' *Melbourne University Law Review*, 38(2), pp 482–524.

Bosland, J. and Townend, J. (2018) 'Open Justice, Transparency and the Media: Representing the Public Interest in The Physical and Virtual Courtroom', *Communications Law*, 23(4), pp 183–202.

Bosland, J. and Townend, J. (2023) 'Reporting Crime in the Wake of the Human Rights Act 1998: Privacy, Criminal Justice and the Media in England & Wales', in A. Roberts, J. Purhouse and J. Bosland (eds) *Privacy, Technology, and the Criminal Process*. Abingdon: Routledge, pp 242–278.

Bosmajian, H.A. (1992) *Metaphor and Reason in Judicial Opinions*. Carbondale: Southern Illinois University Press.

Bowcott, O. and Duncan, P. (2019) 'Half of Magistrates Courts in England and Wales Closed Since 2010', *The Guardian*, 27 January. Available at: https://www.theguardian.com/law/2019/jan/27/half-of-magistrates-courts-in-england-and-wales-closed-since-tories-elected (Accessed: 13 February 2023).

Braun, V. and Clarke, V. (2022) 'Conceptual and Design Thinking for Thematic Analysis', *Qualitative Psychology*, 9, pp 3–26.

Brookman, S. (2021) 'Law Column: 83,000 Reasons to Remember that Arrested Suspects Have Right to Privacy Until Charged', *HoldtheFrontPage*, 12 January. Available at: https://www.holdthefrontpage.co.uk/2021/news/law-column-83000-reasons-to-remember-that-arrested-suspects-have-right-to-privacy-until-charged/ (Accessed: 8 February 2023).

Brooks, T. (ed.) (2019) *Shame Punishment*. London: Routledge.

Bruinsma, G. (2018) 'Classical Theory: The Emergence of Deterrence Theory in the Age of Enlightenment', in D. Nagin, F. Cullen and C. Lero Jonson (eds) *Deterrence, Choice, and Crime*. New York: Routledge, pp 3–28.

Byrom, N. (2019) *Digital Justice: HMCTS Data Strategy and Delivering Access to Justice*. The Legal Education Foundation, pp 1–48. Available at: https://research.thelegaleducationfoundation.org/blog/digital-justice-hmcts-data-strategy-and-delivering-access-to-justice (Accessed: 23 July 2020).

Byrom, N. (2022) 'Anti-Social Behaviour Injunctions are a Great Unknown', *Law Gazette*, 24 August. Available at: https://www.lawgazette.co.uk/commentary-and-opinion/anti-social-behaviour-injunctions-are-a-great-unknown/5113490.article (Accessed: 25 August 2022).

Cairncross, F. (2019) *The Cairncross Review: A Sustainable Future for Journalism*. Online: Department for Digital, Culture, Media & Sport.

Cameron, J. (2020) *Victim Privacy and Open Justice 2.0: At the Frontiers of Change*. 2020 CanLIIDocs 3924. Available at: https://papers.ssrn.com/abstract=4144639 (Accessed: 30 August 2022).

Campbell, D. and Norton-Taylor, R. (2020) 'Human Rights Court Dismisses MI6 Informant Wang Yam's Appeal', *The Guardian*, 16 January. Available at: https://www.theguardian.com/uk-news/2020/jan/16/human-rights-court-dismisses-mi6-informant-wang-yam-appeal (Accessed: 26 August 2022).

Cappelletti, M., Garth, B. and Trocker, N. (1976) 'Access to Justice: Comparative General Report', *The Rabel Journal of Comparative and International Private Law*, 40(3/4), pp 669–717.

Carroll, J. (2014) 'The Jury as Democracy', *Alabama Law Review*, 66(4), pp 825–870.

Centre for Public Data. (2023) Research Paper: Data and Statistical Gaps in Criminal Justice. Available at: https://www.centrefo rpublicdata.org/focus-area-criminal-justice-1 (Accessed: 31 March 2023).

Chamberlain, P., Keppel-Palmer, M., Reardon, S. and Smith, T. (2021) 'It is Criminal: The State Of Magistrates' Court Reporting in England and Wales', *Journalism*, 22(9), pp 2404–2420.

Chan, J.B.L. (1999) 'Governing Police Practice: Limits of the New Accountability', *The British Journal of Sociology*, 50(2), pp 251–270.

Chief Magistrate. (2021) *Guide to the Availability of Live Links in Magistrates' Courts Under their Criminal and Civil Jurisdiction*. Available at: https://www.criminalbar.com/wp-content/uplo ads/2021/01/210126-Live-Link-Matrix-MC-Crime-Civil1.pdf (Accessed: 13 February 2023).

Clark, J. (2021) *HMCTS Remote Hearing Evaluation*, updated 10 December. Available at: https://www.gov.uk/government/ publications/hmcts-remote-hearing-evaluation (Accessed: 13 February 2023).

Cloake, D. (2022) 'Justice Committee Report – A Blogger Responds', *Mouse in the Court*, 2 November. Available at: https://mouseint hecourtroom.wordpress.com/2022/11/02/justice-committee-rep ort-a-blogger-responds/ (Accessed: 8 February 2023).

Colbran, S. (2003) 'The Limits of Judicial Accountability; the Role of Judicial Performance Evaluation', *Legal Ethics*, 6(1), pp 55–72.

Conley, D. and Lamble, S. (2006) *The Daily Miracle: An Introduction to Journalism*, third edn. Oxford: Oxford University Press.

Cornford, T. (2016). 'The Meaning of Access to Justice', in E. Palmer, T. Cornford, A. Guinchard and Y. Marique (eds) *Access to Justice: Beyond the Policies and Politics of Austerity*. Oxford: Hart Publishing, pp 27–40.

Courts and Tribunals Judiciary. (2011) 'Practice Guidance: The Use of Live Text-Based Forms of Communication (Including Twitter) From Court for the Purposes of Fair and Accurate Reporting'. Available at: https://www.judiciary.uk/wp-content/uploads/JCO/Documents/Guidance/ltbc-guidance-dec-2011.pdf (Accessed: 13 February 2023).

Courts and Tribunals Judiciary. (2016) 'Sentencing remarks of Mr Justice Globe, Leeds Crown Court'. Judiciary.uk. Available at: https://www.judiciary.uk/wp-content/uploads/2016/04/sentence-f-d-1.pdf (Accessed: 13 February 2023).

Courts and Tribunals Judiciary. (2021a) 'District Judges (Magistrates' Courts), Courts and Tribunals Judiciary', December 2021. Available at: https://www.judiciary.uk/about-the-judiciary/who-are-the-judiciary/list-of-members-of-the-judiciary/dj-mags-ct-list/ (Accessed: December 2021).

Courts and Tribunals Judiciary. (2021b) 'Transparency in the Family Court Report', 29 October. Available at: https://www.judiciary.uk/guidance-and-resources/transparency-in-the-family-courts-report-3/ (Accessed: 13 February 2023).

Courts and Tribunals Judiciary. (2022) 'Practice Guidance on Remote Observation of Hearings – New Powers', 28 June. Available at: https://www.judiciary.uk/guidance-and-resources/practice-guidance-on-remote-observation-of-hearings-new-powers/ (Accessed: 8 February 2023).

Courts and Tribunals Judiciary. (2023) 'Message from the President of the Family Division: Reporting Pilot in the Family Court', 27 January. Available at: https://www.judiciary.uk/message-from-the-president-of-the-family-division-reporting-pilot-in-the-family-court/ (Accessed: 13 February 2023).

Craig, R. (2019) 'The End of Innocence: Open Justice, Free Speech and Privacy in the Modern Constitution – Khuja (formerly PNM) v *Times Newspapers Limited*', *The Modern Law Review*, 82(1), pp 129–145.

Craig, R. and Phillipson, G. (2021) 'Privacy, Reputation and Anonymity Until Charge: ZXC goes to the Supreme Court', *Journal of Media Law*, 13(2), pp 153–185.

Crow, G. and Mah, A. (2012) *Conceptualisations and Meanings of "Community": The Theory and Operationalisation of a Contested Concept*. AHRC-Funded Connected Communities. Available at: https://www.community-methods.soton.ac.uk/resources/CC%20Final%20Report_30%20March%20GC.pdf (Accessed: 3 July 2023).

Dabhoiwala, F. (2006) 'Summary Justice in Early Modern London', *The English Historical Review*, 121(492), pp 796–822.

Dadomo, C. and Bell, B. (2006) 'Magistrates' Courts and the 2003 Reforms of the Criminal Justice System', *European Journal of Crime, Criminal Law and Criminal Justice*, 14(4), pp 339–365.

Daly, G. and Pattenden, R. (2005) 'Racial Bias and the English Criminal Trial Jury', *The Cambridge Law Journal*, 64(3), pp 678–710.

Davies, N. (1999) 'The decline of the court reporter – Nick Davies', 11 January. Available at: https://www.nickdavies.net/1999/01/11/the-decline-of-the-court-reporter/ (Accessed: 26 July 2022).

Deardon, L. (2022) 'Government has Two Months to Stop Barristers' Strike or Defendants Must be Released', *The Independent*, 28 September. Available at: https://www.independent.co.uk/news/uk/home-news/barrister-strike-uk-prison-government-b2177092.html (Accessed: 13 February 2023).

Donoghue, J.C. (2014) 'Reforming the Role of Magistrates: Implications for Summary Justice in England and Wales', *The Modern Law Review*, 77(6), pp 928–963.

Donoghue, J. (2017) 'The Rise of Digital Justice: Courtroom Technology, Public Participation and Access to Justice', *The Modern Law Review*, 80(6), pp 995–1025.

du Preez, G. (2020) 'Understanding Public Priorities for Criminal Justice', 23 December. Available at: https://www.deloitte.com/global/en/Industries/government-public/blogs/understanding-public-priorities-for-criminal-justice.html (Accessed: 29 June 2023).

Duff, R.A., Farmer, L., Marshall, S. and Tadros, V. (2007) *The Trial on Trial: Volume 3. Towards a Normative Theory of the Criminal Trial*. Oxford: Hart.

Duff, R.A. (2014) 'Towards a Modest Legal Moralism', *Criminal Law and Philosophy*, 8(1), pp 217–235.

Edwards, J. and Simester, A. (2017) 'What's Public About Crime?', *Oxford Journal of Legal Studies*, 37(1), pp 105–133.

Elliott, C. (2014) 'The Readers' Editor On […] The Fallout from a Collision of Child Protection and Open Justice', *The Guardian*, 16 November. Available at: https://www.theguardian.com/commentisfree/2014/nov/16/fallout-from-collision-of-child-protection-open-justice (Accessed: 16 January 2023).

Eltis, K. (2011) 'The Judicial System in the Digital Age: Revisiting the Relationship between Privacy and Accessibility in the Cyber Context', *McGill Law Journal / Revue de droit de McGill*, 56(2), pp 289–316.

Eltis, K. (2016) *Courts, Litigants, and the Digital Age: Law, Ethics, and Practice*, second edn. Toronto, ON: Irwin Law.

Equality Hub. (2022) 'Why we no Longer Use the Term "BAME" in Government', 7 April. Available at: https://equalities.blog.gov.uk/2022/04/07/why-we-no-longer-use-the-term-bame-in-government/ (Accessed: 8 February 2023).

Fair Trials. (2020) *Justice Under Lockdown: A Survey of the Criminal Justice System in England & Wales between March and May 2020.* Available at: https://www.fairtrials.org/articles/publications/justice-under-lockdown-england-wales/ (Accessed: 13 February 2023).

Fair Trials. (2022) *Judicial Review and Courts Bill: Briefing on Automatic Online Conviction and Written Procedure for Indicating Plea.* Available at: https://www.fairtrials.org/articles/legal-analysis/judicial-review-and-courts-bill-briefing-on-automatic-online-conviction-and-written-procedure-for-indicating-plea/ (Accessed: 13 February 2023).

Fairclough, S. (2021) 'The Consequences of Unenthusiastic Criminal Justice Reform: A Special Measures Case Study', *Criminology & Criminal Justice*, 21(2), pp 151–168.

Farrow, T. (2014) 'What is Access to Justice?', *Osgoode Hall Law Journal*, 51(3), pp 957–988.

Ferguson, R.A. (2007) *The Trial in American Life*. Chicago: University of Chicago Press.

Fielding, N. et al. (2020) *Video Enabled Justice Programme: University of Surrey Independent Evaluation*. Available at: https://www.sussex-pcc.gov.uk/our-priorities/access-to-justice/video-enabled-justice-vej/video-enabled-justice-programme-university-of-surrey-independent-evaluation/ (Accessed: 13 February 2023).

Fitz-Gibbon, K. and O'Brien, W. (2017) 'The Naming of Child Homicide Offenders in England and Wales: The Need for a Change in Law and Practice', *The British Journal of Criminology*, 57(5), pp 1061–1079.

Flower, L. (2023) 'Constructing Clickable Criminal Trials: Framing Trials and Legal Professionals in Digital News Reports', *Emotions and Society*, 5(1), pp 48–66.

Fox, J. (2007) 'The uncertain relationship between transparency and accountability', *Development in Practice*, 17(4–5), pp 663–671.

Garvey, S.P. (1998) 'Can Shaming Punishments Educate?', *The University of Chicago Law Review*, 65(3), pp 733–794.

Gauntlett, D., Weaver, C.K. and Carter, C. (2006) 'Ten Things Wrong with the Media "Effects" Model', *Critical Readings: Violence and the Media*. Maidenhead: Open University Press, p 54.

Gibbs, P. (2017) *Defendants on Video – Conveyor Belt Justice or a Revolution in Access?* Transform Justice. Available at: http://www.transformjustice.org.uk/wp-content/uploads/2017/10/Disconnected-Thumbnail-2.pdf (Accessed: 13 February 2023).

Gibbs, P. (2020) 'Written Evidence from Transform Justice'. Available at: https://committees.parliament.uk/writtenevidence/11544/pdf/ (Accessed: 11 May 2023).

Gibson, B. (2009) *The Magistrates' Court: An Introduction*, fifth edn. Hook: Waterside Press.

Gisborne, J., Patel, R., Paskell, C. and Peto, C. (2022) *Justice Data Matters: Building a Public Mandate for Court Data Use*. UK: Ipsos. Available at: https://research.thelegaleducationfoundation.org/wp-content/uploads/2022/07/Justice-Data-Matters-Report-Final-.pdf (Accessed: 7 February 2023).

Godfrey, B., Richardson, J.C. and Walklate, S. (2022) 'The Crisis in the Courts: Before and Beyond Covid', *The British Journal of Criminology*, 62(4), pp 1036–1053.

Gray, D. (2008) 'The People's Courts? Summary Justice and Social Relations in the City of London, c.1760–1800', *Family & Community History*, 11(1), pp 7–15.

Green, D.A. (2021) 'The Last of the Legal Correspondents, and the True Crisis in the Public Understanding of Law', *The Law and Policy Blog*, 3 January. Available at: https://davidallengreen.com/2021/01/the-last-of-the-legal-correspondents-and-the-true-crisis-in-the-public-understanding-of-law/ (Accessed: 26 July 2022).

Greer, C. (ed.) (2010) *Crime and Media: A Reader*. London: Routledge.

Hadjimatheou, K. (2016) 'Criminal Labelling, Publicity, and Punishment', *Law and Philosophy*, 35(6), pp 567–593.

Harrison, S. and Hanna, M. (2022) *McNae's Essential Law for Journalists*, twenty-sixth edn. Oxford: Oxford University Press.

Hart, D. (2014) *What's in a name? The Identification of Children in Trouble with the Law*. Standing Committee for Youth Justice (SCYJ). Available at: https://www.ayj.org.uk/news-content/whats-in-a-name-the-identification-of-children-in-trouble-with-the-law (Accessed: 7 February 2023).

Helm, R. (2021) 'Pleading Guilty Online: Enhanced Vulnerability and Access to Justice', *MLRForum 001*. Available at: https://www.modernlawreview.co.uk/helm-pleading/ (Accessed: 13 February 2023).

Hess, K. and Waller, L. (2013) 'News Judgements: A Critical Examination of Reporting Non-Convictions for Minor Crimes', *Australian Journalism Review*, 35(1), pp 59–70.

Hess, K. and Waller, L. (2016) 'Witness, judge or watchdog?: Journalism and Regional Courts', in A. Harkness, B. Harris and D. Baker (eds) *Locating Crime In Context And Place*. Alexandria, NSW: The Federation Press, pp 120–128.

HMCTS. (2019) 'Media Working Group meeting 16 September 2019 – 16:00 – 18:00'.

HMCTS. (2020) *HMCTS Response And Progress Update On Dr Natalie Byrom Report*, 9 October. Available at: https://www.gov.uk/government/news/hmcts-response-and-progress-update-on-dr-natalie-byrom-report (Accessed: 13 February 2023).

HMCTS. (2022) *HMCTS Video Hearings Service: Guidance for Joining a Hearing*, updated 4 November. Available at: https://www.gov.uk/guidance/hmcts-video-hearings-service-guidance-for-joining-a-hearing (Accessed: 3 July 2023).

HMCTS. (2023a) *Data Governance Panel Formed to Improve Use of Court and Tribunals Data*, 24 January. Available at: https://www.gov.uk/government/news/data-governance-panel-formed-to-improve-use-of-court-and-tribunals-data (Accessed: 13 February 2023).

HMCTS. (2023b) *General Guidance to Staff on Supporting Media Access to Courts and Tribunals*, updated 27 January. Available at: https://www.gov.uk/government/publications/guidance-to-staff-on-supporting-media-access-to-courts-and-tribunals (Accessed: 13 February 2023).

HMCTS. (2023c) *The HMCTS Reform Programme,* updated 24 March. Available at: https://www.gov.uk/guidance/the-hmcts-reform-programme (Accessed: 3 July 2023).

HMCTS. (2023d) *Get Access to HMCTS Data*, updated 24 March. Available at: https://www.gov.uk/guidance/access-hmcts-data-for-research (Accessed: 2 July 2023).

HMCTS. (2023e) *Protocol on Sharing Court Lists, Registers and Documents with the Media*, updated 30 June. Available at: https://www.gov.uk/government/publications/guidance-to-staff-on-supporting-media-access-to-courts-and-tribunals/protocol-on-sharing-court-lists-registers-and-documents-with-the-media-accessible-version (Accessed: 2 July 2023).

Ho, H.L. (2008) 'The Trial on Trial (Vol. 3): Towards a Normative Theory of the Criminal Trial Book Review', *International Commentary on Evidence*, 6(1), pp 1–5.

Hopkins Burke, R. (2014) *An Introduction to Criminological Theory*, fourth edn. Abingdon: Routledge.

Hutton, M. (2019) 'A Labour of Love: The Experiences of Parents of Prisoners and Their Role as Human Rights Protectors', in M. Hutton and D. Moran (eds) *The Palgrave Handbook of Prison and the Family*. Cham: Palgrave Macmillan, pp 385–405.

Jacobson, J., Hunter, G. and Kirby, A. (2015) *Inside Crown Court: Personal Experiences and Questions of Legitimacy*. Bristol: Policy Press.

Jaconelli, J. (2002) *Open Justice: A Critique of the Public Trial.* Oxford: Oxford University Press.

Janes Solicitors. (2016) 'Janes Solicitors' press release on decision of the CCRC to refer the case of Wang Yam to the Court of Appeal', 28 April. Available at: https://www.janes-solicitors.co.uk/news/News/janes-solicitors-press-release-on-decision-of-the-ccrc-to-refer-the-case-of-wang-yam-to-the-court-of-appeal.html (Accessed: 26 August 2022).

Jewkes, Y. (2015) *Media and Crime*, third edn. London: Sage.

Johnston, E. (2020) 'The Adversarial Defence Lawyer: Myths, Disclosure and Efficiency—a Contemporary Analysis of the Role in the Era of the Criminal Procedure Rules', *The International Journal of Evidence & Proof*, 24(1), pp 35–58.

Jones, R. (2021) '"It's the Best Job on the Paper" – The Courts Beat During the Journalism Crisis', *Journalism Practice*, 15(9), pp 1307–1328.

Jones, S. (2021) 'Explaining the Single Justice Procedure in the Magistrates' Court – Inside HMCTS', 26 October. Available at: https://insidehmcts.blog.gov.uk/2021/10/26/explaining-the-single-justice-procedure-in-the-magistrates-court/ (Accessed: 13 February 2023).

JUSTICE. (2018) *Preventing Digital Exclusion from Online Justice*. Available at: https://files.justice.org.uk/wp-content/uploads/2018/06/06170424/Preventing-Digital-Exclusion-from-Online-Justice.pdf (Accessed: 13 February 2023).

JUSTICE. (2019) *One-Year Update – Preventing Digital Exclusion from Online Justice, JUSTICE*. Available at: https://justice.org.uk/one-year-update-preventing-digital-exclusion-from-online-justice/ (Accessed: 13 February 2023).

Justice Committee. (2019) *The Role of the Magistracy: Follow-Up: Eighteenth Report of Session 2017–19*. HC 1654.

Justice Committee. (2020) *Coronavirus (COVID-19): The Impact on Courts: Sixth Report of Session 2019–21*. HC 519.

Justice Committee (2021a) *Oral evidence: The work of the Lord Chief Justice*, HC 868, 16 November. Available at: https://committees.parliament.uk/oralevidence/3022/html/ (Accessed: 10 August 2022).

Justice Committee. (2021b) 'OPJ0006 Written Evidence from Transform Justice'. Available at: https://committees.parliament.uk/writtenevidence/39933/pdf/ (Accessed: 13 February 2023).

Justice Committee. (2021c) 'OPJ0021 Written Evidence from Ed Owen'. Available at: https://committees.parliament.uk/writtenevidence/40141/pdf/ (Accessed: 13 February 2023).

Justice Committee. (2021d) 'OPJ0042 Written Evidence from The Legal Education Foundation'. Available at: https://committees.parliament.uk/writtenevidence/41210/pdf/ (Accessed: 13 February 2023).

Justice Committee. (2021e) 'OPJ0024 Written Evidence from Dr Judith Townend'. Available at: https://committees.parliament.uk/writtenevidence/40163/pdf/ (Accessed: 13 February 2023).

Justice Committee. (2022a) *Open Justice: Court Reporting in the Digital Age: Fifth Report of Session 2022–23*. HC 339. House of Commons Justice Committee.

Justice Committee. (2022b) 'Court System Failing to Support Public Understanding of Justice System', 1 November. Available at: https://committees.parliament.uk/work/1505/open-justice-court-reporting-in-the-digital-age/news/174004/court-system-failing-to-support-public-understanding-of-justice-system/ (Accessed: 6 January 2023).

Justice Committee. (2023) *Open Justice: Court Reporting in the Digital Age: Government Response To The Committee's Fifth Report of Session 2022–23*. House of Commons Justice Committee. Available at: https://publications.parliament.uk/pa/cm5803/cmselect/cmjust/1040/report.html (Accessed: 17 January 2023).

Kahan, D.M. (2006) 'What's really wrong with shaming sanctions', *Texas Law Review*, 84(7), pp 2075–2096.

Kenyon, A.T. and Scott, A. (eds) (2020) *Positive Free Speech: Rationales, Methods and Implications*. Oxford: Hart.

Khadjavi, M. (2018) 'Deterrence Works for Criminals', *European Journal of Law and Economics*, 46(1), pp 165–178.

Kirtley, J.E. (2015) '"Misguided in Principle and Unworkable in Practice": It is Time to Discard the Reporters Committee Doctrine of Practical Obscurity (and Its Evil Twin, the Right to be Forgotten)', *Communication Law and Policy*, 20(2), pp 91–115.

Kitzinger, C. [@KitzingerCelia] *Tweet* (2022) Available at: https://twitter.com/KitzingerCelia/status/1550503855661670400 (Accessed: 26 July 2022).

Kitzinger, C. [@KitzingerCelia] *Tweet* (2023) Available at: https://twitter.com/KitzingerCelia/status/1622956063254364160 (Accessed: 7 February 2023).

Kleck, G., Sever, B., Li, S. and Gertz, M. (2005) 'The Missing Link in General Deterrence Research', *Criminology*, 43(3), pp 623–660.

Koivisto, I. (2022) *The Transparency Paradox*. Oxford: Oxford University Press.

Lageson, S. (2020) *Digital Punishment: Privacy, Stigma & the Harms of Data-Driven Criminal Justice*. New York: Oxford University Press.

Lammy, D. (2017) *An Independent Review into the Treatment of, and Outcomes for, Black, Asian and Minority Ethnic Individuals in the Criminal Justice System*. Gov.uk: London. Available at: https://assets.publishing.service.gov.uk/government/uploads/system/uploads/attachment_data/file/643001/lammy-review-final-report.pdf (Accessed: 27 April 2018).

Law Commission. (2022) 'Contempt of court', *Law Commission of England and Wales*. Available at: https://www.lawcom.gov.uk/project/contempt-of-court-2/ (Accessed: 31 October 2022).

Leader, K. (2021) 'Law, Presence to Absence: The Case of the Disappearing Defendant', in S. Rai, M. Gluhovic, S. Jestrovic and M. Saward (eds) *The Oxford Handbook of Politics and Performance*. Oxford: Oxford University Press, pp 73–88.

Legg, M. and Song, A. (2021) 'The Courts, the Remote Hearing and the Pandemic: From Action to Reflection', *UNSW Law Journal*, 44(1), pp 126–166.

Leveson, B. (2012) 'Hold the Front Page: News-Gathering in a Time of Change', University of Melbourne, 12 December. Available at: https://www.judiciary.uk/wp-content/uploads/JCO/Documents/Speeches/lj-leveson-speech-hold-the-front-page-melbourne-12122012.pdf (Accessed: 26 July 2022).

Livingstone, S. (1996) 'On the Continuing Problems of Media Effects Research', in J. Curran and M. Gurevitch (eds) *Mass Media and Society*, second edn. London: Edward Arnold, pp 305–324.

Long, V. (2021) 'Online Courts: Re-Assessing Inequality in the "Remote" Courtroom', *Excursions Journal*, 11(1), pp 77–102.

Long, V. (forthcoming) 'Social Class in the Magistrates' Courts' (provisional title). Doctoral Thesis, University of Sussex.

Magistrates' Association. (no date) *Becoming a Magistrate*. Available at: https://www.magistrates-association.org.uk/About-magistrates/Becoming-a-magistrate (Accessed: 13 February 2023).

Magistrates' Association. (2019) *Magistrates' Association Comment on the Single Justice Procedure*, 20 August. Available at: https://www.magistrates-association.org.uk/News/magistrates-association-comment-on-the-single-justice-procedure (Accessed: 13 February 2023).

Magistrates' Association. (2022) *Magistrates' Courts and Covid-19*. Available at: http://www.transformjustice.org.uk/wp-content/uploads/2022/04/TJ003_MagCourt_Report_SCREEN.pdf (Accessed: 13 February 2023).

Magistrates' Association. (2023) 'Media Statement: Pausing of Magistrates' Extended Sentencing Powers', Magistrates' Association, 10 March. Available at: https://www.magistrates-association.org.uk/News-and-comments/media-statement-pausing-of-magistrates-extended-sentencing-powers (Accessed: 23 June 2023).

Magrath, P. (2018) 'Transparency, Data Protection and the Law Courts of the Future', *Legal Information Management*, 18(2), pp 70–75.

Magrath, P. and Beresford, G. (2023) *Publication of Listed Judgments: Towards a New Benchmark of Digital Open Justice*. Available at: https://www.iclr.co.uk/blog/news-and-events/publication-of-listed-judgments-towards-a-new-benchmark-of-digital-open-justice/ (Accessed: 28 June 2023).

Malsch, M. and Kaptein, H. (2004) 'Victims on View: Are Victims Served by the Principle of Open Justice?', in *Crime, Victims and Justice*. Abingdon: Routledge.

Marsh, N., McKay, E., Pelly, C. and Cereda, S. (2019) *Public Knowledge of and Confidence in the Criminal Justice System and Sentencing*. UK: Sentencing Council.

Matenaer, P.M. (2021) 'But Instead Expose Them: Public Access to Criminal Trials In U.S. Law And Canon Law', *Wisconsin Law Review*, (4), pp 891–932.

Matthews, R., Hancock, L. and Briggs, D. (2004) *Jurors' Perceptions, Understanding, Confidence and Satisfaction In The Jury System: A Study In Six Courts*. Home Office Online Report 05/04.

McBarnet, D. (1981) 'Magistrates' Courts and the Ideology of Justice', *British Journal of Law and Society*, 8(2), pp 181–197.

McCall, G. J. (1984) 'Systematic Field Observation', *Annual Review of Sociology*, 10, pp 263–282.

McCartney, C. and Shorter, L. (2019) 'Exacerbating Injustice: Post-Conviction Disclosure in England and Wales', *International Journal of Law, Crime and Justice*, 59, pp 1–10.

McClenaghan, M. (2021) 'Open justice? The Closed Doors of Possession Courts', *The Bureau of Investigative Journalism*, 9 November. Available at: https://www.thebureauinvestigates.com/stories/2021-11-09/evictions-open-justice-possession-courts (Accessed: 5 January 2023).

McGill, J. and Salyzyn, A. (2021) 'Judging by the Numbers: Judicial Analytics, the Justice System and its Stakeholders', *Dalhousie Law Journal*, 44(1), p 249.

McGuire, J., Evans, E. and Kane, E. (2021) 'Victim and Witness Retraction and Disengagement: A Systematic Review of Contributing Factors', in J. McGuire, E. Evans and E. Kane (eds) *Evidence-Based Policing and Community Crime Prevention*. Cham: Springer International Publishing, pp 313–359.

McKay, C. (2018) *The Pixelated Prisoner: Prison Video Links, Court 'Appearance' and the Justice Matrix*. London: Routledge, Taylor & Francis Group.

McKeever, G., Royal-Dawson, L., Kirk, E. and McCord, J. (2022) 'The Snakes and Ladders of Legal Participation: Litigants in Person and the Right to a Fair Trial Under Article 6 of the European Convention on Human Rights', *Journal of Law and Society*, 49(1), pp 71–92.

McNamara, L. (2019) 'Closed Judgments: Security, Accountability and Court Processes', *UK Human Rights Blog*, 25 January. Available at: https://ukhumanrightsblog.com/2019/01/25/closed-judgments-security-accountability-and-court-processes/ (Accessed: 2 July 2023).

Ministry of Justice. (n.d.) *Publication Scheme*. Available at: https://www.gov.uk/government/organisations/ministry-of-justice/about/publication-scheme (Accessed: 4 July 2023).

Ministry of Justice. (2020) *Criminal Court Statistics Quarterly: October to December 2019*, 26 March. Available at: https://www.gov.uk/government/statistics/criminal-court-statistics-quarterly-october-to-december-2019 (Accessed: 13 February 2023).

Ministry of Justice. (2021a) *Criminal Court Statistics Quarterly: October to December 2020 (tables)*, 25 March. Available at: https://www.gov.uk/government/statistics/criminal-court-statistics-quarterly-october-to-december-2020 (Accessed: 11 May 2023).

Ministry of Justice. (2021b) *Diversity of the Judiciary: Legal Professions, New Appointments and Current Post-Holders – 2021 Statistics*, 15 July. Available at: https://www.gov.uk/government/statistics/diversity-of-the-judiciary-2021-statistics/diversity-of-the-judiciary-2021-statistics-report (Accessed: 13 February 2023).

Ministry of Justice. (2022a) *The Data First Project: An Introductory User Guide*. Available at: https://assets.publishing.service.gov.uk/government/uploads/system/uploads/attachment_data/file/1056236/data-first-user-guide-version-7.0.pdf (Accessed: 10 February 2023).

Ministry of Justice. (2022b) *Magistrates to Help Tackle Backlog as Sentencing Powers Doubled*, 2 May. Available at: https://www.gov.uk/government/news/magistrates-to-help-tackle-backlog-as-sentencing-powers-doubled (Accessed: 13 February 2023).

Ministry of Justice. (2022c) *Crown Court Sentencing Remarks to be Broadcast for First Time*, updated 28 July. Available at: https://www.gov.uk/government/news/crown-court-sentencing-remarks-to-be-broadcast-for-first-time (Accessed: 13 February 2023).

Ministry of Justice. (2022d) *Criminal Court Statistics Quarterly: April to June 2022, Gov.uk*, 29 September. Available at: https://www.gov.uk/government/statistics/criminal-court-statistics-quarterly-april-to-june-2022 (Accessed: 10 February 2023).

Ministry of Justice. (2023) *Open Justice: The Way Forward*. Available at: https://www.gov.uk/government/consultations/open-justice-the-way-forward (Accessed: 19 June 2023).

Moore S., Clayton A. and Murphy H. (2021) 'Seeing Justice Done: Courtroom Filming and the Deceptions of Transparency.' *Crime, Media, Culture*, 17(1), pp 127–144.

Moran, L.J. (2014) 'Mass-Mediated "Open Justice": Court and Judicial Reports in the Press in England and Wales', *Legal Studies*, 34(1), pp 143–166.

Mulcahy, L. and Rowden, E. (2019) *The Democratic Courthouse: A Modern History of Design, Due Process and Dignity*. London: Routledge.

Mulcahy, L., Rowden, E. and Teeder, W. (2020) *Exploring the Case for Virtual Jury Trials during the COVID-19 Crisis: An Evaluation of a Pilot Study Conducted by JUSTICE*. Available at: https://files.justice.org.uk/wp-content/uploads/2020/04/06165956/Mulcahy-Rowden-Virtual-trials-final.pdf (Accessed: 13 February 2023).

Mullen, P., Collins, C. and Savage, K. (2020) *Understanding and Improving Defendant Engagement*. HMCTS. Available at: https://revolving-doors.org.uk/publications/understanding-and-improving-defendant-engagement/ (Accessed: 13 February 2023).

Nagin, D.S. (2013) 'Deterrence in the Twenty-First Century', *Crime and Justice*, 42, pp 199–263.

Nel, F. and Milburn-Curtis, C. (2021) 'Down, but not Out: Journalism Jobs and Media Sustainability in the UK', in T. Marjoribanks et al. (eds) *Journalists and Job Loss*. London: Routledge, pp 171–183.

O'Carroll, L. (2014) 'Phone Hacking: *Wall Street Journal* Wins Ruling on Reporting Restrictions', *The Guardian*, 17 January. Available at: https://www.theguardian.com/media/2014/jan/17/phone-hacking-trail-wall-street-journal (Accessed: 8 February 2023).

OGN UK (Open Government Network UK). (2022) 'UK Warned It Could be Declared "Inactive" by Open Government Partnership', 22 August. Available at: https://www.opengovernment.org.uk/2022/08/25/the-uk-warned-it-could-be-demoted-by-open-government-partnership-joining-malta-malawi-and-el-salvador/ (Accessed: 5 January 2023).

Oliver, L. (2010) 'What was "First" about Tweeting from the Julian Assange Bail Hearing?', *Journalism.co.uk*, 15 December. Available at: https://blogs.journalism.co.uk/2010/12/15/what-was-first-about-tweeting-from-the-julian-assange-bail-hearing/ (Accessed: 6 February 2023).

Owen, E. (2021) OPJ0021 Written Evidence. 11 November. Available at: https://committees.parliament.uk/writtenevidence/40141/pdf/ (Accessed: 13 February 2023).

Owusu-Bempah, A. (2016) *Defendant Participation in the Criminal Process*. London: Routledge.

Owusu-Bempah, A. (2020) 'Understanding the Barriers to Defendant Participation in Criminal Proceedings in England and Wales', *Legal Studies*, 40(4), pp 609–629.

Parliament.uk. (2023) *Magistrates: Sentencing: Question for Ministry of Justice. UIN 176590, Tabled on 29 March 2023*. Available at: https://questions-statements.parliament.uk/written-questions/detail/2023-03-29/176590 (Accessed: 23 June 2023).

Pickett, J.T. (2018) 'Using Behavioral Economics to Advance Deterrence Research and Improve Crime Policy: Some Illustrative Experiments', *Crime & Delinquency*, 64(12), pp 1636–1659.

Porter, A. (2019) 'Prosecuting Domestic Abuse in England and Wales: Crown Prosecution Service "Working Practice" and New Public Managerialism', *Social & Legal Studies*, 28(4), pp 493–516.

Public Accounts Committee. (2023) *Progress on the Courts and Tribunals Reform Programme*. HC 1002. London: House of Commons Committee on Public Accounts.

Purshouse, J. (2016) 'The Reasonable Expectation of Privacy and the Criminal Suspect', *The Modern Law Review*, 79(5), pp 871–884.

Purshouse, J. (2020) '"Paedophile Hunters", Criminal Procedure, and Fundamental Human Rights', *Journal of Law and Society*, 47(3), pp 384–411.

Purshouse, J. (2021) 'The Automatic Identity Suppression of Criminal Suspects', Birmingham: Criminal Law Reform Now Network.

Quick, O. (2006) 'Prosecuting "Gross" Medical Negligence: Manslaughter, Discretion, and the Crown Prosecution Service', *Journal of Law and Society*, 33(3), pp 421–450.

Reed, L. (2020) 'Transparency Review Call for Evidence Closes – Our Response', *The Transparency Project Blog*, 11 May. Available at: https://transparencyproject.org.uk/transparency-review-call-for-evidence-closes-our-response/ (Accessed: 13 February 2023).

Reed, S. (2022) 'The Tories have Broken Britain's Justice System – Labour Can Fix It', *New Statesman*, 22 September. Available at: https://www.newstatesman.com/politics/labour/2022/09/steve-reed-conservatives-uk-justice-system-labour (Accessed: 13 February 2023).

Robertson, G. (2012) 'A Great Tradition of Open Justice', in J. Townend (ed.) *Justice Wide Open*, pp 9–11. Available at: https://openaccess.city.ac.uk/id/eprint/1926/ (Accessed: 28 June 2023).

Robins, J. (2020) 'We Need To Protect Open Justice During The Covid-19 Emergency', *The Justice Gap*, 29 May. Available at: https://www.thejusticegap.com/we-need-to-protect-open-justice-during-the-covid-19-emergency/ (Accessed: 8 September 2022).

Robins, J. and Newman, D. (2021) *Justice in a Time of Austerity*. Bristol: Bristol University Press.

Rossner, M. and Tait, D. (2023) 'Presence and Participation in a Virtual Court', *Criminology & Criminal Justice*, 23(1), pp 135–157.

Rowbottom, J. (2018) *Media Law*. Oxford, UK: Hart Publishing.

Rowden, E. (2013) 'Virtual Courts and Putting "Summary" back into "Summary Justice": Merely Brief, or Unjust?', in J. Simon, N. Temple and R. Tobe (eds) *Architecture and Justice*. Abingdon: Routledge.

Rozenberg, J. (2011) 'Judges Will Decide Who can Tweet from Court', *The Guardian*, 14 December. Available at: https://www.theguardian.com/law/2011/dec/14/judges-decide-who-tweets-from-court (Accessed: 8 August 2022).

Rozenberg, J. (2021a) 'Two Legal Correspondents Retire', *A Lawyer Writes*, 4 January. Available at: https://rozenberg.substack.com/p/two-legal-correspondents-retire (Accessed: 13 February 2023).

Rozenberg, J. (2021b) 'Automating the Criminal Courts', *A Lawyer Writes*, 27 July. Available at: https://rozenberg.substack.com/p/automating-the-criminal-courts (Accessed: 13 February 2023).

Sang, B. (2004) 'Choice, Participation and Accountability: Assessing the Potential Impact of Legislation Promoting Patient and Public Involvement in Health in the UK', *Health Expectations*, 7(3), pp 187–190.

Schlesinger, P. and Tumber, H. (1994) *Reporting Crime: The Media Politics of Criminal Justice*. Oxford: Clarendon Press.

Scott, P.F. (2016) 'An Inherent Jurisdiction to Protect the Public Interest: From PII to "Secret Trials"', *King's Law Journal*, 27(2), pp 259–275.

Shnoor, B. and Katvan, E. (2019) '"A perfect façade?": Transparency, Honor and Judicial Scarce Resources', *International Journal of the Legal Profession*, 26(1), pp 143–158.

Simson Caird, J. and Bartlett, G. (2017) The Prisons and Courts Bill: Court Reform. House of Commons Briefing Paper 7907.

Smith, T. et al. (2022) *'An Endlessly Strange Experience': Experiences Of Media Reporting on Criminal Courts During the Covid-19 Pandemic*. Available at: https://uwe-repository.worktribe.com/output/9655419 (Accessed: 27 July 2022).

Speer, J. (2012) 'Participatory Governance Reform: A Good Strategy for Increasing Government Responsiveness and Improving Public Services?', *World Development*, 40(12), pp 2379–2398.

Spilsbury, M. (2018) *Journalists at Work*. National Council for the Training of Journalists (NCTJ). Available at: https://www.nctj.com/wp-content/uploads/2021/08/JaW-Report-2018-web.pdf (Accessed: 13 February 2023).

Stacey, C. (2015) 'Unlock Speak at ICO Policy Conference: "The Google Effect – Criminal Records and the 'Right to be Forgotten'"', *Unlock*, 11 November. Available at: https://unlock.org.uk/unlock-speak-at-ico-policy-conference-the-google-effect-criminal-records-and-the-right-to-be-forgotten/ (Accessed: 15 July 2022).

Stacey, C. (2017) 'Rehabilitation in the Internet Age: The Google-Effect and the Disclosure of Criminal Records', *Probation Journal*, 64(3), pp 269–275.

Susskind, R (2019) *Online Courts and the Future of Justice*, first edn. Oxford: Oxford University Press.

Syal, R. (2022) 'Suella Braverman to Consider Giving Anonymity to Suspected Criminals', *The Guardian*, 3 October. Available at: https://www.theguardian.com/politics/2022/oct/03/suella-braverman-to-consider-giving-anonymity-to-suspected-criminals (Accessed: 5 October 2022).

Tambini, D. (2021) 'What is Journalism? The Paradox of Media Privilege', *European Human Rights Law Review*, 2021(5), pp 523–539.

Temkin, J. and Krahé, B. (2008) *Sexual Assault and the Justice Gap: A Question of Attitude*. Oxford: Hart.

Terpstra, J. and Fyfe, N.R. (2015) 'Mind the Implementation Gap? Police Reform and Local Policing in the Netherlands and Scotland', *Criminology & Criminal Justice*, 15(5), pp 527–544.

Terry, M., Johnson, S. and Thompson, P. (2010) *Virtual Court Pilot Outcome Evaluation*. Ministry of Justice Research Series 21/10.

The Guardian. (2022) 'The Guardian View on Privacy Law and Press Freedom: Failing to Strike a Balance', *The Guardian*, 18 February. Available at: https://www.theguardian.com/commentisfree/2022/feb/18/the-guardian-view-on-privacy-law-and-press-freedom-failing-to-strike-a-balance (Accessed: 8 February 2023).

The Swindon Advertiser. (2019) *Why do Local Newspapers Report On Court Cases and What are we Allowed To Publish?*, *Swindon Advertiser*. Available at: https://www.swindonadvertiser.co.uk/news/17644216.local-newspapers-report-court-cases-allowed-publish/ (Accessed: 10 February 2023).

Thomas, C. and Balmer, N. (2007) 'Diversity and Fairness in the Jury System in England and Wales', *Ministry of Justice Research Series*: 02/07.

Thornton, B. (2016) 'More than Half of Local Newspapers Don't Have a Court Reporter', *The Justice Gap*, 25 October. Available at: https://www.thejusticegap.com/half-local-newspapers-dont-court-reporter/ (Accessed: 17 April 2019).

Thornton, B. (2017) 'The Mysterious Case of the Vanishing Court Reporter', *The Justice Gap*, 7 April. Available at: https://www.thejusticegap.com/mysterious-case-vanishing-court-reporter/ (Accessed: 17 April 2019).

Thurman, N., Cornia, A. and Kunert, J. (2016) *Journalists in the UK*. Oxford: Reuters Institute for the Study of Journalism.

Torrible, C. (2022) 'Trust in the Police and Policing by Consent in Turbulent times', *Safer Communities*, 21(3), pp 171–183.

Townend, J. (2013) 'Closed Data: Defamation and Privacy Disputes in England and Wales', *Journal of Media Law*, 5(1), pp 31–44.

Townend, J. (2019) 'Why we need a national commitment to open justice data', *UK Open Government Network*, 10 October. Available at: https://www.opengovernment.org.uk/2019/10/10/why-we-need-a-national-commitment-to-open-justice-data/ (Accessed: 18 October 2019).

Townend, J. and Wiener, C. (2021) *'Justice System Data': A Comparative Study*. The Legal Education Foundation. Available at: https://research.thelegaleducationfoundation.org/research-learning/funded-research/justice-system-data-a-comparative-study (Accessed: 23 July 2021).

Townend, J. and Magrath, P. (2021) 'Remote Trial and Error: How COVID-19 Changed Public Access to Court Proceedings', *Journal of Media Law*, 13(2), pp 107–121.

Townend, J. (2023) 'How to Translate the Principle of Open Justice Into Reality – Reflections on the Justice Committee's Report', *Communications Law*, 28(1), pp 37–42.

Transform Justice. (2017) 'How Can Justice be "Seen to be Done" in an online system?', *Transform Justice*, 10 February. Available at: https://www.transformjustice.org.uk/how-can-justice-be-seen-to-be-done-in-an-online-system/ (Accessed: 13 February 2023).

Transform Justice. (2021) 'Computer Says Yes – You Will Pay a Fine and Get a Criminal Record', *Transform Justice*, 27 August. Available at: https://www.transformjustice.org.uk/computer-says-yes-you-will-pay-a-fine-and-get-a-criminal-record/ (Accessed: 13 February 2023).

Tyler, T.R. and Huo, Y.J. (2002) *Trust in the Law: Encouraging Public Cooperation with the Police and Courts*. New York: Russell Sage Foundation.

Tyler, T.R. (2003) 'Procedural Justice, Legitimacy, and the Effective Rule of Law', *Crime and Justice*, 30, pp 283–357.

Ugwudike, P. (2015) *An Introduction to Critical Criminology*. Bristol: Policy Press.

UKPCA. (no date) 'The UK Press Card Authority'. Available at: https://presscards.co.uk/the-uk-press-card-authority/ (Accessed: 23 August 2023).

Van de Merwe, A. (2017) 'Victims and the Media', in *Routledge Handbook on Victims' Issues in Criminal Justice*. Abingdon: Routledge.

Van de Walle, S. (2009) 'Confidence in the Criminal Justice System: Does Experience Count?', *The British Journal of Criminology*, 49(3), pp 384–398.

Waller, L. and Hess, K. (2011) 'The Pillory Effect: Media, The Courts and the Punitive Role of Public Shaming in Australia', *Media and Arts Law Review*, 16(3), pp 229–240.

Walters, M. et al. (2017) *Hate Crime and the Legal Process: Options for Law Reform*. Brighton: University of Sussex. Available at: http://sro.sussex.ac.uk/id/eprint/70598/ (Accessed: 13 February 2023).

Warby, M. (2020) 'Judicial Oversight of Judicial Data Processing an English Perspective', *Yearbook of Estonian Courts*. Available at: https://aastaraamat.riigikohus.ee/en/judical-oversight-of-judical-data-processing-an-english-perspective-1/ (Accessed: 7 February 2023).

Ward, J.R. (2017) *Transforming Summary Justice: Modernisation in the Lower Criminal Courts*. Abingdon: Routledge.

Welsh, L., Skinns, L. and Sanders, A. (2021) *Sanders & Young's Criminal Justice*, fifth edn. Oxford: Oxford University Press.

Welsh, L. (2022) *Access to Justice in Magistrates' Courts*. Oxford: Hart Publishing.

Wilkins, T. (2022) *Protecting Local Justice, Young Fabians*. Available at: https://www.youngfabians.org.uk/protecting_local_justice (Accessed: 13 February 2023).

Woods, L., McNamara, L. and Townend, J. (2021) 'Executive Accountability and National Security', *The Modern Law Review*, 84(3), pp 553–580.

Young, R. (2013) 'Exploring the Boundaries of the Criminal Courtroom Workgroup', *Common Law World Review*, 42(3), pp 203–239.

Index

References to endnotes show
both the page number and the note number (231n3).

D

K

L

M

N

O

P

R

Printed and bound by CPI Group (UK) Ltd, Croydon, CR0 4YY

15/09/2026

14962385-0002